Free to Be Me!

May God's grace
help you become
that special person
He made you to be.

Love in Jesus,
Mark A. Pearsont

Also by Mark A. Pearson
　Christian Healing: A Practical, Comprehensive Guide
　"Gifts of Healing" in *The Gifts of the Spirit*
　The Basics of the Faith
　Boot Camp for Christians

Mark A. Pearson is president of the Institute for Christian Renewal, an interdenominational teaching and healing ministry, and co-founder and chaplain of New Creation Healing Center, a whole-person ministry bringing together medicine, Christian counseling and prayer. Pearson has a graduate degree in theology from Oxford University, England, and a doctorate from Boston University. He is married to Dr. Mary Grace Pearson, and they have three adult children.

Free to Be Me!

Mark A. Pearson

SPIRE

© 1992 by Mark A. Pearson

Published by Fleming H. Revell
a division of Baker Book House Company
P.O. Box 6287, Grand Rapids, MI 49516-6287

Spire edition published 2001

Previously published by Chosen under the title *Why Can't I Be Me?*

Printed in the United States of America

All rights reserved. No part of this publication may be reproduced, stored in a retrieval system, or transmitted in any form or by any means—for example, electronic, photocopy, recording—without the prior written permission of the publisher. The only exception is brief quotations in printed reviews.

ISBN 0-8007-8694-7

Unless otherwise indicated, Scripture quotations are from the HOLY BIBLE, NEW INTERNATIONAL VERSION®. NIV®. Copyright © 1973, 1978, 1984 by International Bible Society. Used by permission of Zondervan Publishing House. All rights reserved.

Scripture quotations identified KJV are from the King James Version of the Bible.

For current information about all releases from Baker Book House, visit our web site:

                http://www.bakerbooks.com

This book is dedicated to my wife
Mary Grace E. Pearson, D.O.

Acknowledgments

❖ I wish to thank several people who have been instrumental in this book. First is Patience Webb, who first made me aware of the world of personality type. Her quiet cheerleading got me hooked. Then there is Jane Campbell, editor of Chosen Books, who sold the idea of this book to her superiors. Jane, besides being a helpful editor, is also a good friend. Becoming a good friend is John Sherrill, who carefully edited the manuscript. If the reader can more easily understand this book, thank John for his insisting on a liberal dose of clarifying sentences. In addition I thank Mary Shelton for her wise counsel, especially when I was writing the inner healing chapter of my first book, but also at a few critical places in this book. Thanks go, too, to Ann McMath for helpful suggestions in the final editing of the manuscript.

Lastly, thanks especially to "my readers," five very different people who read through several versions of the manuscript while it was being revised: The Rev. Jürgen W. Liias, associate rector, Church of the Advent, Boston, Massachusetts; the Rev. Janice H. Miller, an Episcopal deacon and former missionary to China,

Acknowledgments

now living in Sanford, Florida; the Rev. J. Douglas Sholl, American Baptist pastor and clinical counselor at Wellspring Health Ministries, Inc., Biddeford, Maine; the Rev. Armand L. Weller, United Church of Christ pastor and executive director of the Biblical Witness Fellowship, now residing in Chesapeake, Virginia; and Dr. Mary Grace Pearson, physician and wife. Without Mary in my life, I would not have delved as deeply into the Myers-Briggs Type Indicator. And without the insight that the Myers-Briggs Type Indicator provides on getting along with people of very different personality types, Mary and I would have killed each other long ago!

Contents

	Introduction	13
1	Your Wounded Personality	21
2	Personality Type Theory	29
3	Wounded Personalities	57
4	Healing Your Wounded Personality	75
5	Communicating with Opposites	97
6	Working Better in a Group Setting	133
7	Growing in Christ through Understanding Personality Type	154
	Epilogue: How to Make Your Church Personality-Friendly	203
	Appendix 1: Releasing Anger, Pain and Judgment—Healing Relationships for Christians	207
	Appendix 2: Objections to Personality Type Theory	209
	Bibliography	218
	For Further Information	223

The Personality Types

Extravert—Outgoing, likes the world of people and action
Introvert—Quiet, likes the inner world

Sensate—Literal, likes details, the precise and routine
Intuitive—Imaginative, good brainstormer, can see the big
        picture

Thinker—Dispassionate, makes decisions based on the rules
Feeler—Compassionate, makes decisions based on the
        heart

Judge—Predictable, likes structure, order, plans
Perceiver—Flexible, likes spontaneity and informality

Introduction

❖ There has been an explosion of interest lately in three fascinating subjects: personality type, inner healing and Christian spirituality.

And why not? It is fun to understand what makes us tick. It is important to investigate any legitimate avenue to emotional health. And it is vital to learn about the various ways we can best express our commitment to Jesus Christ. Go to any bookstore and note the number of books on these three subjects. Yes, there is interest.

This book is different in that it brings together these three subjects—personality type, inner healing and Christian spirituality. In other words, an individual is happy and fulfilled when his or her personality is affirmed, and miserable and disoriented when it is not. He or she can enjoy the emotional freedom inner healing brings, or stay locked in woundedness. He or she can find the way to walk with God and work for God that is just right, or let the relationship with Him remain distant and any efforts in ministry unfruitful. Personality type studies, inner

Introduction

healing prayer and spiritual direction are crucial to individual growth.

The recent popularity of *personality type studies* comes from two rather different sources. First are the writings of Tim LaHaye. Using the ancient Greek four temperament theory (sanguine, choleric, melancholy and phlegmatic), LaHaye looked at the significant differences each personality has from the others and how God can use each in His service. In his book *Transformed Temperaments,* he illustrated how God's plan for our growth in maturity is not for us to cast aside our individual personalities, if that were even possible, but for Him to transform them by the Holy Spirit. This book, along with his other similar books, has brought hope to many people who wondered if God could love, much less use, individuals like themselves.

Second is the Myers-Briggs Type Indicator®*. Within the past decade, thousands of churches have been hosting personality type workshops using the Myers-Briggs Type Indicator, usually abbreviated MBTI®*. This popular method of studying personality—more than one million people take the Myers-Briggs questionnaire each year—has its roots in the clinical studies of Swiss psychologist Carl Gustav Jung. (Be sure to take a look at "Objections to Personality Type Theory," Appendix 2, page 209.)

This typology looks at personality from four dimensions: One's posture to the outward world (extravert/introvert), the manner in which one gathers and weighs data (sensate/intuitive), how one makes decisions (thinker/feeler), and how one relates to closure

* MBTI and Myers-Briggs Type Indicator are registered trademarks of Consulting Psychologists Press, Inc.

and order (judge/perceiver). The popularity of the MBTI stems in part from its practical applications to counseling, career choice and job satisfaction, management styles, teaching methods, spiritual growth and other aspects of life.

Inner healing or healing of memories was first made popular by Agnes Sanford, a housewife, Bible teacher and wife of an Episcopal priest. She asserted that most of us carry painful memories of events of the past, whether consciously or unconsciously, and these memories negatively influence our thoughts, feelings, actions and relationships.

Many of the emotional wounds we suffer come from childhood. Childhood is when we form our beliefs about whether or not the world is safe for us, whether or not people are trustworthy, whether or not we have worth to God, ourselves and others. How we are treated by others—parents, siblings, teachers, church leaders—goes far to mold our attitudes toward ourselves, other people and God. In her book *Breaking Free When You're the Adult Child of an Alcoholic,* Christine Adams puts it this way: "Healthy parents impart positive messages to their children—messages about love, security, acceptance, discipline, guidance, independence, protection, faith. Through their words and actions, normal parents say, 'You are lovable.' "

The Bible exhorts us to train up a child in the way he should go, and when he is old, he will not depart from it (Proverbs 22:6). But what if our parents were not healthy, or what if we were not trained up in the way we should go? Then what? If we were the victims of our parents' own problems, or if we were trained according to lies, we will grow up wounded.

Dr. David Seamands notes that a child who has been repeatedly put down, ridiculed or hurt in some deep way grows up to be an adult who has difficulty in relating to others in a healthy way. This makes sense. If an adult trained up in the way he ought to go will not depart from it in adulthood, someone trained up in the way he should *not* go will probably not depart from that either, that is, until God intervenes in some way.*

While it is not possible to rewrite history, it is possible through the ministry of inner healing to let the grace of God remove the present-day harmful consequences of the painful experiences of the past. Since Agnes Sanford began teaching on the subject of inner healing, hundreds of books have been published and tens of thousands of retreats and services have been conducted applying this branch of the healing ministry to the hurts of God's people.

Spiritual direction is a ministry that assists us in discovering which of the various ways of spiritual expression are best suited to us and helps us grow in them. This is important, for trying to follow someone else's spirituality can be, at best, a stifling experience. We will look at this in depth in chapter 7.

Is This Book for You?

The ministry of inner healing deals with hurts that run along the spectrum from simple to deep and foundational.

For purposes of discussion, let's look arbitrarily at both ends and the middle point of this spectrum noting the severity of the hurt, its effect and how a person might respond.

* Seamands believes that this unhealthy way of relating is manifested in four different attitudinal/behavioral patterns. He has identified these as the hurting child, the hating child, the humiliated child and the horrified child. Any of David Seamands' books is well worth reading. His description of the four kinds of wounded children comes from his book *Putting Away Childish Things.*

Level of Hurt	What Happens	The Response
Annoying event	One takes a frightening or negative comment to heart	To stay clear of, or be upset by, reminders of that event; hurt feelings
Wounding of personality	One is not allowed to own or express true personality; ridiculed regularly for it	To become inhibited; to be unsure of identity; to feel uncomfortable in broad areas of daily living
Severe abuse	Not just personality but one's whole core being is violated sexually, physically, psychologically, or all three	To take on the various roles from a dysfunctional home; possibly psychosis, promiscuity or frigidity in some, mistrust of people, self-loathing, multiple personalities, suicide, pathological behavior, etc.

As for simple hurts, these, while painful, are not systemic. Here is an example.

A subplot in one of the episodes of the television series "Father Dowling Mysteries" was Father Prestwick's fear of going to the zoo. When he was four, a zoo animal snatched away his ice cream cone and that frightening memory kept the good father

Introduction

from enjoying zoos ever since. This story illustrates one focus of the ministry of inner healing—painful but not earth-shattering memories. Although God can and does heal problems like this one, a person can live a full, rich life and never go to the zoo.

Far more serious, however, are those problems so devastating that persons are affected in every aspect of who they are. Such damage might come from growing up in an alcoholic or otherwise seriously dysfunctional family, being physically or sexually abused, and the like.

Everything within such persons is twisted and broken. No aspect of their lives is left unaffected. Mature relationships, appropriate behavior and an enjoyable walk with the Lord are difficult if not impossible until major healing occurs at the very center of their beings. A growing body of Christian literature on the various aspects of abuse and a growing number of people practicing Christian psychological counseling are working to help these individuals.

But what about those in the middle, those people whose problems are more serious than Father Prestwick's but less serious than those whose entire beings have been twisted? During my eighteen years of ordained ministry I have been asked by hundreds of people this question: "What about me? I don't need lengthy therapy, but my problem is more than something a ten-minute chat in the hall or a brief prayer will solve. Isn't there anything for me in this ministry of inner healing?" If you feel this way, this book is for you.

I will deal with the healing of woundedness that, while serious, is not at the core of your being. I will also examine the healing of this woundedness in how you express yourself to others and live in relationship to the world. I call this *the healing of wounded personality*.

Free to Be Me!

1

Your Wounded Personality

❖ We have been hearing a lot lately about people who have problems in adulthood because they were mistreated in childhood. The words *codependent, adult child of an alcoholic, sexually molested* and *dysfunctional family* are becoming commonplace on the talk shows and in books. These words all describe various forms of serious abuse of a person, abuse that can twist and distort that person's core being.

But there is another kind of disorder that, while more subtle, nevertheless touches many people. It can seriously affect your relationships with others, hamper your enjoyment of life, harm your relationship with God and keep you from feeling at home with yourself. It is the problem of wounded personality.

What do I mean by the term *personality*? For the purposes of this book I will define *personality* as "one's unique mental and emotional disposition, that special way of expressing oneself to others and orienting oneself, inwardly and outwardly, to the world." In other words, personality is how you *express* your essential being. Personality is not that core being itself, which has to do with your values, beliefs, commitments.

It is important to make this distinction. People of the same personality type can have very different core values. (An extravert could be a Christian or an atheist or a Muslim.) And people of the same core values can have very different personalities. There is no one personality type that is more Christian than another. Christians are found among people of every personality type.

The study of personality is fascinating and important, given its ramifications for society. We should not be surprised, therefore, to realize that thinkers throughout the ages have turned their attention to differences in human personality.

You do not have to be a philosopher, of course, to be confronted with differences in personality. In virtually every family there are people with personalities markedly different from each other. In some families these differences are recognized and valued. A mother of eight once told me, "I love all my children equally, but I treat each one differently, because each one is a unique individual with his or her own special traits, interests, contributions and needs." In families like this one the best of these individual characteristics is brought out. Family members are proud of the rich diversity that their family possesses and they honor each member for who he or she is. Family members recognize that each personality type has its own particular ways of expressing human weakness. Discipline is given more to correct than to punish, to help, not embarrass, and with love, not ridicule.

In other families, however, differences are not recognized, or, if they are, they are not appreciated. A person's individuality is seen as a negative. It is often deemed odd or put down as a sign of rebelliousness—or at least a lack of conformity to certain standards that are deemed important. Sometimes this lack of acceptance is shown through meanness and may take the form of deliberate emotional mistreatment. It can be wrapped up in the evil of pathological behavior. Rejecting a person on the basis of personality is often indicative of a great insecurity or desire for control or power on the part of the person doing the rejecting.

In still other families, it is not meanness but misplaced love that is the basis for rejecting. The desire is to train the child to be virtuous, but the definition of what is good is extremely narrow, far more narrow than what God expects. This is one of the pitfalls of so-called legalistic Christianity, with its humanly devised list of rules, regulations and taboos. Like the Pharisees of biblical times, legalistic Christians are so concerned with obedience they forget grace. In their desire to obey God they often play God with those committed to their charge. In homes where respectability and reputation are given excessive priority, young people may be forced into a straitjacket of proper behavior so as to make the right impression on others. Sadly, so many grow up learning to wear a mask—presenting themselves to others on the basis of the expectations of others—that they lose awareness of what they themselves are really like. One woman shared with me, "I know what my mother would want me to say and do, but I no longer know what I want to say and do."

It may be very difficult with people raised in homes or churches like this to acknowledge that they have some serious problems in adulthood. In the same way, it may be very difficult for an adult whose personality was wounded because of misplaced love to find out the root cause of what is wrong. When I told a friend that much of his emotional distress could be traced to his parents, he told me, "That can't be true! They were always wonderful to me." In one sense, he is right. His parents were, and still are, very loving. Their motives were the best. But in trying to raise their son to be a responsible, good adult, *they squeezed him into a mold.* In that squeezing, they did him harm.

Part of what his parents were doing was trying to teach him right from wrong. Not only was that an appropriate thing for his parents to do, it was their responsibility. Unfortunately, however, they did much more than that. They tried to force him to express appropriate Christian values in one particular way, unaware that other ways of expression—including their son's— were also appropriate.

Specifically, this was a clash over loudness. These parents were prim and proper. They also happened to be introverts. As Christians, they felt it part of proper Christian deportment to be polite. So far so good. But they then went on to define politeness as being prim, gentle and softspoken. In doing this they confused style with virtue. It was bad enough to force this on themselves, but when they also imposed their ideas on their extravert son it left him wounded. "It's gotten so bad," he once told me, "that every time I forget and talk or laugh loudly, I have this feeling deep in my soul that I have offended God."

In yet other families, the desire to be loving gets wrapped up in the unhealed emotional woundedness still remaining in one or both parents. If a parent was not valued in childhood for who he or she was, that confusion will, in turn, get passed on to the next generation.

The example of one's own parents is the most significant teacher of how to be a parent. If they were not comfortable with their own personality, it will be difficult for them to make their children comfortable. If they are insecure, that insecurity is sometimes compensated for by insisting that others conform to whatever is familiar and safe.

In some cases, no lasting damage is done. While chafing under their parents' lack of acceptance of who they are, some children find the affirmation they need in their friends, teachers or clergy, or in a personal relationship with the Lord. Because they sense God's loving acceptance and are able to receive the acceptance of other people, they grow up with a fairly good self-esteem, while perhaps counting the days until they can move out of the family home.

One woman said to me, "When I was a teenager, my mother kept putting me down for being interested in helping homeless people. She thought they were homeless because they deserved to be. So I stopped telling her I was volunteering at the soup kitchen and told her instead I spent my time after school with friends. While Mom never valued my caring for hurting people, my friends at the soup kitchen did. I continue my volunteer work to this day and feel good for doing so. I guess Mom will just never understand."

In some instances, growing up in a home with little esteem for different personality types can actually lead to flexibility in later life. One man told me, "I was raised by two very orderly, plan-ahead kind of parents, although by nature I am very spontaneous. They were exasperated with me for being the way I was. Now that I'm on my own, I have the freedom to be spontaneous; but what my parents kept drilling into me makes it more possible for me to fit in at work where there are procedures and deadlines." Thanks be to God when people suffer no lasting harm by being raised in a home where individual personality is not valued!

Many times, however, the experience is not so positive. The lack of affirmation has led to wounding. These individuals cannot become the persons their parents want them to be—it just isn't who they are. If that were not enough, they feel guilty about being who they really are. Because they have never been allowed to grow into a mature version of their individual personalities, when they do act more true to themselves they act in an awkward

Free to Be Me!

manner, like someone trying to write with the opposite hand. They are, in effect, trapped in a pseudo-personality, a sort of personality no-man's land, not able to be what others want, but not free to be themselves. The Swiss psychologist Carl Gustav Jung wrote that every person has an innate predisposition to develop certain personality characteristics. If your family accepts you, you will develop naturally in a certain way. If it does not, you may find it difficult to know who you really are as a person.

Gershen Kaufman, a clinical psychologist and a professor at Michigan State University, understands the problem that emerges when our personalities are not accepted as being one of shame. In his book *Shame: The Power of Caring,* Kaufman says, "Contained in the experience of shame is the piercing awareness of ourselves as fundamentally deficient in some vital way as a human being. To live with shame is to experience the very essence or heart of the self as wanting."

Conrad Baars, M.D., calls the problem *deprivation neurosis.* Those who did not receive affirmation of who they really are will fear others, yet desperately need and seek their approval.

Wounded personality, a sense of shame, deprivation neurosis—however we label the problem, it is one from which many people need to be set free. Before we move on in our exploration, let's look at three classic examples. As with every story in this book, the names have been changed to protect the identities of the people involved.

Gina grew up a quiet, introvert girl in a very loud and energetic Italian family. Every Sunday after mass at St. Anthony's her aunts, uncles and cousins all came over for dinner. And every week the same thing happened. After about a half hour of being with her family, Gina was drained emotionally and retreated to her room to read. Noticing her absence, her parents would go looking for her and make her rejoin the party. "Your Uncle

Rocco hasn't seen you in a week! Your Aunt Philomena wants you to tell her about your school project. Don't be so aloof from the family that loves you. Come downstairs until the company goes."

While her parents were, in their minds, trying to make Gina sensitive to the feelings of her family and socially well-behaved, the effect on Gina was wounding. She wanted to be with them. She loved not only Uncle Rocco and Aunt Philomena, but all her family very much. But when she was with them for a while she got a headache! She couldn't act the way her parents wanted her to, and she couldn't get them to understand why she fled to her room. She wondered if there was something terribly wrong with her. Until she was healed, Gina was a terribly unhappy person.

Then there was Paul, a rather mystical, creative teenager in a family of engineers. His family could not understand, much less appreciate, Paul's "daydreaming." They continued to exhort him to study hard and prepare for a "real" career and not the one he wanted in art. While Paul's best friend, Scott, a similar kind of person in a similar kind of family, was somehow able to satisfy his family's desires and still develop his artistic bent, Paul could not. While believing deep down that his real calling was to be an artist, Paul internalized enough of his family's values to attend—and flunk out of—three engineering schools. In addition, his personality woundedness manifested itself in a failed marriage and a reputation for being the black sheep of the family.

Paul felt guilty whenever he tried to work on his art. "Whenever I tried," he told me, "it was as if I could hear somebody in the family say, 'There's that dreamer again. Let's hope he doesn't have to go through an economic depression like we did.' " At the same time, Paul could never get good enough at engineering. Until Paul was healed he just drifted through life sideways.

It is not always parents who create the problem. Any primary person in your life, anyone who has a significant influence on you, can be the source of emotional woundedness. Teachers or church leaders, for example, can help your personality develop or can harm it.

Marcy is an orderly, structured person who attended a nondenominational church where the worship was offered spontaneously as the people felt the Holy Spirit lead them. While Marcy believed that the Holy Spirit can, and often does, lead people to read from Scripture, pray, give a word of prophecy or start singing a certain song, she wondered if everything she experienced in her church was actually the Spirit at work. *Doesn't the Bible also talk about doing things decently and in order?* she wondered. *Can't the Holy Spirit be at work in the planning of a well-ordered service, too?*

The leaders of her church taught regularly that the other churches in town were just following forms rather than letting worship flow from the heart. There was, thought Marcy, some truth to that. She also felt that the pastors of her church had helped her spiritually in many ways. She was left unable to enter into the worship of her church the way she wanted to, yet emotionally blocked from attending another church. Until she was healed, Marcy never felt comfortable at the worship services of any church.

In this book we will see how people in these and other situations received healing. We will look at a number of categories of personality type and the strengths and weaknesses of each. Following that, we will examine how we might inflict wounds on ourselves as well as others. We will explore a number of healing steps, including ways to build bridges. Finally, we will look at the various ways a Christian can legitimately express his or her faith.

Let's get started.

2

Personality Type Theory

❖ From ancient times to today, people have noticed differences in personality. We notice, for example, how some people are outgoing while others are more reserved, or how some people tend to be emotional while others are cool-headed. We notice that some enjoy detailed work while others prefer generalities. While only a few of us have studied personality type theory in any detail, we all know from observation that people are different.

Hippocrates (460–370 B.C.), besides being the father of medicine, can also be described as the father of personality type theory. He noted four temperaments: the sanguine, the melancholic, the choleric and the phlegmatic—each dependent, he believed, on the humors of the body (blood, black bile, yellow bile and phlegm). The four-temperament theory was popularized in Europe in the eighteenth century by the German philosopher Immanuel Kant. Since that time, there has been an explosion in interest in personality theory, due in part to the relatively new science of psychology.

Behind the scientific and theoretical studies of personality are the needs of people to understand themselves and others, and to use these understandings to make life better. The work that is under way to study human differences is important. The diversity of personality types can be a source of rich blessing; but it can also be a source of confusion and conflict. If the insights of personality type theory are true, we can learn how to overcome some of this confusion and conflict and be in a position to see people of different personalities as people with complementary gifts.

This was certainly the case for my wife and me when we were dating. Mary, a physician by training, would speak with a scientist's exactness. Her language was literal and precise. I, on the other hand, would speak in the generalized, symbolic terms well-suited to a clergyman who is also a writer and musician. We were nearly spending more time trying to figure out what each other meant in a conversation than actually having the conversation! It seemed there were walls where we hoped there could be bridges. By reading some helpful literature on personality type theory and using it as a tool for relationship building, we were able to turn liabilities into assets and potential areas of conflict into areas of rich complementarity.

One of the most widely used instruments in the area of personality type theory today, and the one that proved to be so helpful to Mary and me, is the Myers-Briggs Type Indicator®, abbreviated MBTI®. The development of the MBTI began in the 1910s with Katharine Briggs. Briggs developed a typology of personality based on patterns she found in biographies. She identified people as either meditative, spontaneous, executive or sociable. In 1923, she read the newly translated version of Carl Jung's book *Psychological Types*. It gave her a much fuller picture of what was becoming a fascination. For the next twenty years Briggs and her daughter Isabel Myers were avid type-watchers and refined their theories.

During World War II, Myers sought to apply her theories to the assigning of personnel to the war effort. She reasoned that people would work with greater productivity and enjoyment if their work better matched their temperament. Although seemingly sensible, her theories were not widely accepted, partially because she and her mother were women, non-psychologists and non-academics. In addition, among the psychology establishment, measurement of personality was considered a dubious enterprise. Nevertheless, individuals in the worlds of education and of psychology, starting with just a few people in the early 1960s, began to give acceptance and support. Myers continued to work to refine her theories and provide for a personality measuring device for individuals, something that Jung did not provide. That device was named the Myers-Briggs Type Indicator.

The MBTI, depending on which version is used, asks more than one hundred questions about preferences in situations drawn from daily life. The questions are written in a style called forced choice—that is to say, you are forced to choose between two, occasionally three, given answers. You might be asked, for example, Does following a schedule (A) appeal to you, or (B) cramp you? The MBTI is especially appealing because there are no right or wrong answers. The questions deal with personality, not morality. Liking or disliking schedules does not make a person better or worse than another. Thus, the tool is non-threatening and an enjoyable, safe way to learn about yourself and others.

Note that the Myers-Briggs Type Indicator does not claim to be an infallible measurement device, nor should it ever be assumed that the results of the MBTI are the definitive description of your personality type.

There are several reasons for this. For one thing, no testing device, obviously, is one hundred percent perfect. Second, the way you answer the questions may be subtly influenced by your emotional state at the time. Let's suppose, for example, you have just had an argument with your boss over the untidiness of your desk. You take the MBTI questionnaire early that evening and come across a question having to do with tidy desks. You may answer the opposite of what you really feel, either because you are afraid of your boss and thus accept his value judgments or because you are trying to get back at your boss by giving not your answer, but the one that your boss would not like!

Another reason why your answer may be different from that of your true self is because of woundedness. You may have been reared to see one of the answers as being "Christian." Thus, even though the questions are value-free, subconscious messages from your childhood force you to choose a particular answer whether it describes you or not.

So should you take the Myers-Briggs Type Indicator, take its assessment of your personality type with a grain of salt. It is a helpful tool, but not an infallible one. Read carefully through the descriptions of personality type, which are given in great detail in the Myers-Briggs literature, and, with the help of people who know you well, draw tentative conclusions about your personality.

In more than 75 percent of the cases the results of the MBTI and the conclusion a person makes about his or her personality type are identical. In most of the rest of the cases there is only a slight difference, usually in only one of the four variables. It does not matter so much, ultimately, that you know what precise personality type you are. What is important is to gain insight into yourself and into how different personalities interact.

In 1975, the Center for Applications of Psychological Type was organized as a research organization for the MBTI. Since that time a professional association for MBTI users was formed, the Association for Psychological Type, of which I am a member. It publishes a scholarly journal in MBTI research and applications, the *Journal of Psychological Type*. At present the MBTI is one of the most widely used personality measurement tools available and applications of MBTI theory make significant contributions in the areas of interpersonal relations, team-building, education, counseling, job placement, management and leadership, and spiritual growth.

Because of the vocabulary used in the Myers-Briggs questionnaire, few people under high school age can take it successfully. The new Murphy-Meisgeier Type Indicator (Palo Alto, California: Consulting Psychologists Press) has a reading level of grades three through six, thus enabling the personality type of children to be measured.

I heartily encourage you to take the Myers-Briggs Type Indicator for a more precise measuring of your personality type. It will open up a wonderful world of discovery for you. In the meantime, you can make tentative conclusions about your personality type by reading the descriptions listed below.

Four pairs of words describe various aspects of personality. Pick the one word in each of the four pairs that better describes you. In some cases it will be easy. You are very much that kind of person and hardly at all like the opposite. In other cases, it won't be so easy because you are almost equally both. In still other cases you may find that you are one way at work and a different way at home. My purpose in this book is not to give a complete description of personality type but to delineate differences in personality so as to help facilitate healing.

According to the MBTI, then, here are the four personality types. Described by word-pair opposites, these are: extravert/introvert, sensate/intuitive, thinker/feeler and judge/perceiver.

Extravert/Introvert

This first set of personality types describes *our relationship to the world around us*.

The extravert likes the world of people and action. He or she wants to be where people are and where things are happening. The extravert derives energy from such outer stimulation and finds solitude fairly quickly to be draining. Usually, though not always, the extravert is gregarious and enjoys talking. He or she thinks things through by talking with others. Often the extravert will lament, "I wish I hadn't said. . . ." An extravert will often have many relationships, though not many deep ones.

I remember an extravert saying, with all seriousness, "I'm throwing a party for a hundred of my closest friends." This is because an extravert relates easily to the realm of people and action, and not so much to that quiet, inner place of depth. Not knowing that place well, it is often difficult for the extravert to invite another person to share it.

Introverts, and extraverts whose extraversion is not very strong, often think of extraverts as shallow. This is not necessarily the case. It is just that everything that goes on in an extravert's head—insights of genius, fleeting notions of lunacy and the process of thinking things through—is shared out loud for everyone to hear. If the listener is one who keeps most of those thoughts to him or herself, the assumption is that everything the extravert shares is of equal value and, therefore, this person is shallow and not very bright.

Personality Type Theory

The introvert likes the world within. He or she best enjoys solitude and finds it strengthening. While able to enter into the outer world of people and public activities, the introvert finds these to be draining and longs for a place that is quiet and low-key. He or she generally thinks things through internally. The introvert's lament is more likely to be, "I wish I had said. . . ."

While many introverts are shy and withdrawn—this is certainly what many people think the word *introvert* means—this is not always the case. Many introverts are actually good at human relationships because these are learned, not innate, skills. The introvert will reveal him or herself more slowly. Usually, though not always, the introvert talks less frequently and in a much gentler way. The introvert keeps his or her inner thoughts a secret and finds superficial chitchat and breaking the ice with new people difficult.

Relationships usually develop slowly, but once an introvert senses another person might prove to be a true friend, then he or she will open up, often more deeply than an extravert. Should that other person, indeed, prove to be respectful of an introvert's private space, the introvert will often invite the caring person to that special secret inner world he or she so values. The friendships enjoyed in that place are often very deep.

Because they do not share as readily with most people (except for their special friends), introverts are often misunderstood. People tend to judge others on the basis of what is seen, and since introverts do not present as much for public view, it is often assumed that they have little to offer.

For any number of reasons, many people marry persons of the opposite personality type. People like ourselves are familiar, safe and easily understood. We need opposites to be challenged and to grow. And people of a different personality type are mysterious, often a major attraction in affairs of the heart.

While this difference of personality can be a source of enrichment for those who value the diversity, it can also be a source of conflict, especially once the novelty of difference has worn off. Personality type is so much a part of us that we seldom think about it. We often assume other people are the same. Other people's differences are not seen as *basic* differences, just as idiosyncrasies that are no longer amusing after a while.

Helen, a laid-back person, put it, "Richard's spit-and-polish style was different at first and rather refreshing. Then I told him that it was time to get serious about our relationship. He could drop the soldier act as it was getting old. He told me it was no act!"

It sometimes comes as a surprise when we discover that otherwise normal people may see things in a radically different way or have an attitude to the world that is significantly different from our own. Let me illustrate both the differences in personality types and how these differences tend to manifest themselves in daily life with two examples.

Charles and Martha attended social functions often because of Charles' job. For Charles, an introvert, going to these events was a burdensome duty. He would much rather have had a few close friends over to their house. For Martha, each event was another chance to meet a whole variety of fascinating people. While she seldom got to know any of them in depth, she found their company to be stimulating and the conversation informative.

Conflict often arose between Charles and Martha when they had been at one of these events for about an hour. Charles felt that he had fulfilled his social obligation and it was time to go home. Talking with a variety of people had drained him and now he wanted to retreat to the solitude of his home to recharge his batteries. He wasn't a party pooper; he was pooped by the party!

Martha, meanwhile, was just warming up. She had not yet spoken to a number of the people there. She was afraid she would miss something if she left so early. She didn't dislike staying at home, but she wondered why anyone would rather be all cooped up when there was something exciting going on.

Another couple, Gretchen and Bill, were devout Christians but they were having trouble finding a church that suited them both. Gretchen, an introvert, believed a worship service should follow the injunction to "Be still and know that I am God." She longed to worship God in a sort of holy silence. She liked to go to church and sit quietly before the service began. Chatting was for coffee hour afterward. The service should lift her to the holy presence of God, she felt, not mimic a band concert.

Bill, an extravert, wondered if Gretchen had ever read the psalmist's exhortation to "make a joyful noise unto the Lord." Why should we cheer at football games, Bill wondered, but just mumble under our breaths to the Lord of the universe? If you can't get excited about God, who or what should you get excited about?

While all of us have moments when we are more the extravert and moments when we are more the introvert, we tend to be more one than the other, some of us very much so. So let me ask you these questions: Of the descriptions above, which one are you more like? When you need to recharge your batteries or find that favorite place when you are stressed or worried, do you head to people or to solitude?

Sensate/Intuitive

This has to do with *where we find and how we gather the information needed for making decisions or forming conclusions.* It also involves *how a person relates to details.*

Free to Be Me!

A sensate, as the name implies, is a person who is oriented toward the five senses of sight, smell, touch, hearing and taste. Such a person tends to notice details usually with a high degree of accuracy. As Yogi Berra once put it, "It's amazing what you can observe just by watching." As a result, a sensate tends to be more precise and literal, sometimes missing the forest for the trees, but definitely seeing the trees.

Routine procedures do not usually trouble the sensate. A sensate places great emphasis on reality and recognizes life for what it is. He or she identifies with Sergeant Joe Friday's interest in "just the facts, ma'am." A sensate will not budge until he or she is convinced of the truth of something. While sensates preserve society's values, they are sometimes closed to new insights or new ways of doing things.

An intuitive, on the other hand, tends to be a deep blue sky person, relying on hunches or speculative ideas rather than on specific data. He or she is excellent at brainstorming sessions where all kinds of possibilities are brought out. An intuitive can also see more deeply into people and situations, although sometimes his or her insight is not accurate.

While the routine tends to bore the intuitive, he or she does not find complexity overwhelming. An intuitive can see the figurative and symbolic underneath surface details and wants to know the meaning and significance of things. He or she tends also to anticipate what might happen in the future, to wonder what might be. Because of this, and because an intuitive does not grasp specific factual details nearly as well as a sensate, an intuitive tends to be an idealist. An intuitive is open to new ideas, sometimes to the point that freedom to think whatever he or she wants is valued more than the truth.

Since the so-called Enlightenment (which began around 1650), knowledge based on intuition has been devalued. The general belief since that time has been that no knowledge can be trusted except the mathematical or scientific; all other knowledge is just opinion or hunch.

In terms of personality type this stacks the deck against the intuitive, just as in terms of religion, it stacks the deck against Christianity. Needless to say, the inability to approach core Christian doctrines—the virgin birth, the Incarnation, the Resurrection—from a scientific standpoint makes them, for some, impossible to believe. C. S. Lewis pointed out, however, that such skepticism does not come from a careful examination of the facts, but from ruling out miracles because of a simplistic way of determining what the truth is.

Fortunately, we are starting to see the return to an earlier view that we can gain knowledge in a number of ways besides mathematical or scientific, and that these ways are not illogical but simply express a different kind of understanding.

I remember when I was being trained to administer the Myers-Briggs Type Indicator. The sensates and the intuitives were placed in different rooms with cans of Tinker Toys and told to make a building. After we were all finished we looked at the building the opposite group made.

The sensates made a building that was, to some of us intuitives, rather boring and utilitarian. It lacked any creativity of style or beauty. It would, however, likely withstand a nuclear bomb blast, so precise was the engineering!

The building we intuitives came up with was, if I may say so myself, a work of art. Our imaginations went wild and we came up with something creative. It would have added to the decor of any room had not a sensate walked up to it and blown it over with one puff! The point was well made: Both personality types had strengths and weaknesses. We needed each other to make something functional *and* beautiful.

Barbara and Lloyd found themselves increasingly at odds with each other over their church's midweek Bible study and its leader, Fred. Barbara, a sensate, felt that Fred was taking too many liberties with the text. "It says what it means and it means what it says," she insisted. "He brings in so many different meanings to the text it has become the word of Fred, not the Word of the Lord."

Lloyd, an intuitive, wasn't so sure. "How can you give an engineer's definition of such words as *love, peace* and *joy?* Aren't they subjective things? If that is the case, can't you say that any of the words of Scripture can mean a whole variety of things?" And so their dispute went.

Once again, while we all have both sensate and intuitive aspects, each of us tends to be more one than the other. Ask yourself the question: Am I more a person who likes details but not the big picture, or do I come up with the big vision and grow impatient with details?

Thinker/Feeler

This has to do with *the basis on which a person makes decisions* and *the way he or she weighs things in coming to a conclusion*. It does not mean that a thinker has no feelings or that a feeler cannot think. A thinker usually exercises concern for people in a less emotional, more general way. A feeler thinks, but with the heart.

A thinker tends to value principles and rules. He or she knows that the basis of a well-ordered society is a set of carefully crafted laws and procedures, the observance of which benefits all. The thinker knows that the basis of justice is to treat people fairly and equally; thus decisions should be made objectively. A thinker will seldom abandon the truth (however that truth is understood) but will hold to it with steadfastness. He or she believes that because God gave us minds, decisions can and should be logical and principled. A thinker, especially if also an intuitive, readily looks to the future to anticipate problems that might arise.

Although sometimes this makes the thinker appear to be hardhearted or cold, this is not necessarily the case. Rather, by being dispassionate in dealing with people, the thinker tries to respect the dignity of all. In doing so the thinker may actually be more loving than a feeler who sometimes will respond—with great feeling—to just the one or two persons before him or her while failing to grasp problems elsewhere. It was often said about former President Ronald Reagan, who appears to be a strong feeler, that he would give you the shirt off his back while signing a bill that would make it likely that the poor would lose their shirts. Whether this was true of him or not, the point is illustrative: Feelers tend to respond to the person in need but do not necessarily relate to more abstract concepts like poverty and justice.

A feeler tends to make decisions on the basis of human considerations. He or she knows that there are always exceptions to rules and that one must be very careful lest a law crush an individual. A feeler knows that behind logical considerations there are emotional ones, too. He or she is greatly troubled when there is not harmony or unity and may sacrifice principle to achieve these. A feeler understands that each person is unique and each situation is different and that this transcends anything more fixed or impersonal. Sympathy and compassion are important words to the feeler. As a result, the feeler tends to be a bleeding heart and can, in being susceptible to a tale of woe, actually hurt people by affirming their wrong choices. At his or her best, however, a feeler brings love and warmth to people who are hurting.

I suppose political fairness demands we also pick on a Dem-

Free to Be Me!

ocrat! You may remember the television debate between George Bush and Michael Dukakis in which Bernard Shaw of CNN asked Governor Dukakis what he would do if someone raped Kitty. To the astonishment of virtually everyone, instead of responding to the turmoil of his wife in such a scenario and the various emotions welling up in his heart, Dukakis gave an arid, intellectual response about the systemic problems contributing to crime in America! Analysis revealed that this turned off millions of people. There is a place for cool, logical analysis of the problems in America and the careful crafting of wise, just responses, but not when your wife has just been attacked! If President Reagan's feeler function worked at the expense of his logic, Governor Dukakis' thinker function got in the way of his humanity.

The difference between a thinker and a feeler was dramatically illustrated for me one day. I was attending a conference when, during a break, the baby of one of the conference participants somehow got locked in a closet.

The thinkers in the group responded to the event in machine-like fashion. I almost expected a robot voice to say, "Problem: baby in closet. Our task: liberate baby." They seemed unaware of the emotional needs of the baby's mother, who by now was quite distraught. Their response was to accomplish a task, not soothe a person.

Meanwhile, the feelers were responding to the mother's emotional distress and bringing words of reassurance that, no, she wasn't a bad mother because her baby somehow got locked in a closet. The feelers were at their best caring for an individual who was hurting. In fact, they were so attentive to the mother's emotional needs that had it not been for the presence of those thinkers, the baby might still be in the closet!

A difference of style was apparent between Bob and Ted, two clergymen at a particular church. While not disagreeing on theology or morality, it was clear that that they had a difference in approach. Bob's preaching style was to unfold in a precise and clear manner the moral teachings of Scripture. Some in the congregation liked that because it challenged them to obey their Lord. Others preferred the approach of Ted who tended to emphasize how God loves us all. "Ted is giving people easy outs to disobey God and hurt themselves and others," some in the congregation said. "Bob is chewing people up with his stern moralism," others replied.

The apostle Paul told the Ephesians (chapter 4, verse 15) to speak the truth in love. While this balance is to be desired, the fact is we tend to lean either toward the truth side or the love side of any particular equation. While we may never individually achieve that balance, as we link up with others we can keep each other from going into extremes and minister in balance.

Ask yourself this question: While acknowledging that one is not better or more godly than the other, do I tend more to respond to a situation with the objective standards in mind or with the exception that breaks the rules?

Judge/Perceiver

These terms have to do with *the relative like or dislike of structure, planning, order and conclusion.* Here especially we need to note that the use of some terms in personality type literature is different from their use in everyday speech. The word *judge* does not mean that the person is necessarily judgmental, nor does the word *perceiver* mean he or she is necessarily more observant than others.

The judge tends to be structured. He or she tends to plan the work and work the plan. The judge usually has a good idea of where things are going and does not take to surprises well. He or she tends to get upset when an opportunity is lost because of lack of follow-through. A judge likes things to be decided. If you hear the phrase "Let's get this show on the road," it likely is coming from a judge. While a judge can have fun and play (although usually in the form of achieving or competing), he or she likes to work. A judge likes to get one project finished before starting another. A judge can be controlling.

The perceiver likes things to be relatively unstructured. He or she tends to like things left open, always ready to take in new information or to change plans should something come up. The perceiver resists being pushed to make a decision, meet a deadline or follow a precise procedure. The perceiver might be described as informal or last-minute. Two key words describing the perceiver are *spontaneous* and *flexible*. He or she does not fret when something that could have happened didn't, because something else will always turn up. While perceivers can get the job done (although not always according to procedure or on time), they enjoy play. "Enjoy life" and "Let's wing it" are a perceiver's mottoes. The perceiver can drift from the focus or not take responsibilities seriously.

Joan and Doris had the responsibility of leading worship for their church's midweek healing service. While both took their task seriously, it was apparent that their differences in approach were causing friction between them. Joan, a perceiver, believed that they should not plan anything until the day of the service. "That way we can respond both to the specific needs of the congregation and to whatever world events are unfolding. Why pick the Scripture readings and the songs way ahead and have them out of sync with what's happening?" she said.

Doris, a judge, believed that while they could always make a few last-minute changes if urgently necessary, God was not limited to inspiring a person at the last minute. "God planned the coming of the Messiah for a long time," she insisted. "He can certainly help us with plans a few weeks ahead. Besides, that way we will have a balanced diet of themes, carefully chosen, and not be subject to the whims of the moment."

There are few perceivers who cannot plan at least some things, and few judges so locked in that they are totally inflexible. And yet, there are differences between the two. Let me ask: Do you tend to wait until the last minute and hang loose on structure, or do you plan in advance and pretty much stick to your plans? Are you comfortable or uncomfortable with a lack of structure? Do you feel threatened or relieved by schedules?

I hope these descriptions and illustrations have adequately conveyed the differences in personality type. As you looked at four different personality pairs—extravert/introvert, sensate/intuitive, thinker/feeler and judge/perceiver—you have probably identified with one half of each of the word pairs more than the other. You may have decided, for example, "I'm more an extravert (E) than an introvert (I), more an intuitive (N) than a sensate (S), very much more a feeler (F) than a thinker (T), and more a judge (J) than a perceiver (P), though not by very much. I guess I am an 'ENFJ' person." In most Myers-Briggs literature a person is described in terms of such combinations of letters. (If you would like to learn more about each of the sixteen different personality types the combinations of letters represent, and for further reading, consult the bibliography at the end of this book. I also urge you once again to consider taking the Myers-Briggs Type Indicator if you haven't already.)

Let me expand for a minute on the point that your personality can be better understood not just by looking at one of the descriptions in a word pair, but by seeing how all four aspects of personality mesh together. To make it easier, instead of looking at a four-personality-trait combination (like the example of the ENFJ person, above), let's look just at two.

To do this, let me quote from Professor Gary Harbaugh and his book *God's Gifted People*. Like many others who write about the Myers-Briggs Type Indicator, Harbaugh points out the value of looking at the middle two letters (taken from the sensate-intuitive and thinker-feeler categories). Believing that different personalities are as much gifts from God as those gifts listed in Scripture (like healing and prophecy), he describes these personality types in this way:

Sensate-thinker (ST) has the *gift of practicality* and is well-suited for living in the here and now; he or she brings stability, asks *why* questions and handles technical tasks well.

Sensate-feeler (SF) has the *gift of personal helpfulness* and is well-suited to reach out and lift people up; he or she notices things about people and attends to details for the sake of others.

Intuitive-thinker (NT) has the *gift of looking ahead* and is well-suited to let the future guide the present; he or she is inquisitive and can face changes logically and analytically, helping people scope out possibilities and see the big picture.

Intuitive-feeler (NF) has the *gift of possibilities for people* and is well-suited to keeping hope alive; he or she is insightful and idealistic, always searching for possibilities that can help others.*

As you might imagine, the four different personality traits can combine either to strengthen or moderate each other. A sensate tends to be a guardian of traditional ways because until there is a preponderance of concrete new evidence, there is no reason to change. A thinker tends to make decisions based on objective truths. Put these together as a sensate-thinker (ST) and you have

---

* Gary Harbaugh, *God's Gifted People* (Minneapolis: Augsburg Fortress, 1988).

a person who is going to stand firm in society and in the Church for the assured verities of traditional values.

An intuitive tends to experiment with new ideas. In fact, exploring the possibilities is one of the intuitive's favorite activities. A feeler tends to make decisions based on personal values, especially in response to a person perceived to be hurting. Put those together as an intuitive-feeler (NF) and you have a person who tends to sit lightly on received truths, especially when they seem to restrict, confine or, especially, oppress people.

At face value, there is nothing wrong with either personality combination. Once again, these are God-given. But they do have dangers. The ST is in danger of oppressive legalism. The NF is in danger of permissive license. Neither an ST nor an NF personality is any better than the other, although a person hurt by one may be blind to the dangers of the other. The problem develops when you are not aware that a biblical balance is needed. When one or the other becomes extremist and gains power, disaster can ensue.

I knew a man once who exemplified the dangers of an ST orientation gone too far. He was a nice enough person, gentle, well-mannered. But quickly you learned that there was no give with him. There was always a right way to do everything. He wasn't nasty or offensive in showing me the correct way to do things, nor was he often wrong in what he put forth as the correct way. As a result, I did not notice at first that there was a problem. But after several weeks of being around him I finally said, "Don't you ever make a mistake?"

"Well, not very often," he replied. "I think things through carefully and look at all the facts before I set out to do something. As a result there isn't much chance for error. If I do make a mistake, I examine it so it won't happen a second time."

Once again, he wasn't trying to be arrogant; he had just concluded there was no reason to do things wrong if one can do them right. The trouble was, he had little understanding for those who failed. I shared with him the plight of a friend of mine. There was no condemnation for her in his response, but there was no compassion, either. He wasn't a bad man, this ST extremist, but I noticed that his only friends were people who shared his views.

One can go to the extreme in an NF direction as well. I read an article recently written by a woman who had demanded freedom of choice (an NF tendency) over against any restrictions on what she should do or think. She had worked hard to demand her rights on every conceivable issue, and she was quick to sound the alarm against any system of doctrine or morality. She felt that to love people meant to affirm them, and affirmation meant to let them do whatever they wanted. As an expression of this, she approved of her teenage children's right to be sexually active, even inviting them to let their boyfriends or girlfriends spend the night in their bedrooms.

But gradually events changed her mind. She had become aware of the bad results taking place in her own life, in the lives of her children and in society because of permissiveness and the emphasis on personal rights at the exclusion of responsibilities and duties. She thought it through and concluded that personal and societal happiness rests on loving but firm regulation of human behavior, based on the revealed truths of the Christian faith.

She concluded that we are happier and freer not when our minds soar in flights of speculative fancy, but when they figure things out correctly; not when our hearts turn love into permissiveness, but when they discipline, regulate and guide with love and understanding. No, she did not want a dictator state, but she did want to warn her like-minded friends that unregulated freedom was the slippery slope to bondage.

So, it is important to understand that the way the various

aspects of personality come together makes each of us the individuals we are, with our own particular strengths and weaknesses.

We need to recognize another factor as well: the relative intensity of any one of the traits. Often the words *strong* or *moderate* are used to describe a particular personality type designation, as in, Gretchen is a moderate intuitive, or, Leroy is a strong sensate.

This means, in Gretchen's case, that while she is an intuitive, she is not much more an intuitive than a sensate. Perhaps she functions as an intuitive sixty percent of the time and a sensate forty percent of the time. Or else she functions as an intuitive most of the time but not in a very pronounced way. As a result, she might be rather adaptable, able to be either a sensate or intuitive as the situation warrants. In addition, Gretchen may be able to serve as a bridge between strong intuitives and sensates.

Being in the middle can be a disadvantage. Gretchen may, for instance, be unsure how to proceed in a certain situation. She might vacillate between the two different ways of acting or thinking. She also may not be able to function with the conviction or power that someone who is stronger in either of these traits usually does.

As for Leroy, the strong sensate, he functions as a sensate most of the time. It is his gift and he knows it well. When it is called for, it can help the cause, whatever that may be. His opposite, or intuitive, side so seldom manifests itself that, when it does, Leroy is unsure how to use it. It can, therefore, be a source of difficulty. Because Leroy does not use it very often, it is weak and undeveloped. Its use might not be very accurate or effective. Leroy might just embarrass himself with it or else have difficulty understanding those with that expression of personality.

Just a few more words on strong and moderate personality. A

Free to Be Me!

person may be strong in some of the four Myers-Briggs scales and moderate in others. And, we must not place value judgments on the words *strong* and *moderate*. They have nothing to do with having strength of character or with being ethically vacillating. The terms refer to personality type, not moral integrity.

Another aspect to the understanding of personality type is the concept of shadow. Many believe that as we approach midlife other aspects of our personalities come to the surface. Some refer to these less seen aspects as the shadow. Some call it the other side.

Basically, they mean those aspects of personality type that are not dominant. If you are an extravert, then introversion would be your shadow side, and so on in each of the other three categories. When you were a child or young adult this shadow side popped up its head from time to time, but as you get older it may start to emerge in a more pronounced way.

In some schools of psychology the shadow means something quite different. It refers to a murky, rather sinister underside to who we are, perhaps even the repressed drives to think or do evil. That's not what I mean here.

Let's briefly look at a few issues having to do with the shadow.

First, becoming aware of your shadow side can be a wonderful opportunity for enrichment. Sometimes the shadow can be fun. Its occasional emergence on its own may be an interesting curiosity; or using it deliberately may be an amusing diversion.

I am a strong intuitive with a very weak shadow sensate function. I enjoy balancing my checkbook, a detailed, precise sensate activity. I enjoy it because it is different from what I normally do. Since most of what I do—writing, preparing sermons and lectures—engages my dominant intuitive function, for me to stop what I am doing and engage in the sensate task of balancing the checkbook is like playing. But God forbid that I should become an accountant, spending forty hours a week keeping detailed financial ledgers accurate to the penny. It would be asking me to spend too much of my time functioning in a way that is not my normal dominant self.

As you get older, more of your shadow will emerge. If you are comfortable with who you are, the emergent shadow becomes a source of personal enrichment. New possibilities open up. You have a greater understanding of what makes others tick. Those who can receive the blessings of the emerging shadow are better able to reach out to new people and situations.

Second, trying to act in your shadow personality can make you humble before the Lord. Acting in the shadow personality can make you feel weak and incompetent. Those who are proud and used to being in control feel threatened by it. Like a child learning to ride a bicycle, you will likely feel unsure and make many mistakes. But if your greatest desire is to serve the Lord, the emergence of the shadow can be an opportunity to humble yourself before Him. Here is a prayer for guidance: "I feel weak and vulnerable when functioning in this shadow personality, Lord. I want to use whatever blessings may come from this to Your honor and glory and the extending of Your Kingdom. I need Your help in developing these new aspects of who I am so I will not bring You dishonor."

Along these lines, sometimes it is easier to see our "unsanctified" sides better through the shadow personality than the dominant one. The reason for this is simple. We have had many years to work on our obvious negatives. By the grace of God and our efforts in spiritual growth we have made progress in holiness in many aspects of our attitudes and behavior. As for the rest, we have had a number of years to wallpaper over them! Although they still exist, they are covered over with politeness and denial. But we have not had that opportunity with the sins of our shadow sides. We are so busy trying to cope with this unusual way of thinking or acting, we don't have too much energy for putting on a veneer.

In other words, the sins of the shadow side are not any more in number than the sins of the dominant side. It is just that we have not worked on them nearly as much. If we are wise we will use the sins that emerge when we are in our shadow as opportunities for humility before the Lord and for working further on spiritual maturity with His help. That is why the apostle Paul would boast of his weaknesses—so that he would remain humble and reliant on God's grace (2 Corinthians 12:9).

Third, too much time spent in activities that demand working in the shadow, not dominant, personality can cause burnout. Many people believe that burnout does not come as much from working too hard as it does from working in the wrong kind of work, work that is not suited to the personality. (In fact, one of the practical uses of the Myers-Briggs Type Indicator is to help suggest to people in the process of changing jobs what kinds of jobs might be more suited to their personalities.) I can work for hours preparing sermons and lectures. Although I sometimes get physically tired from this, seldom does it cause me serious stress. Were I to become an accountant, as I suggested earlier, I would probably burn out fairly quickly.

Now working in a job for which you are temperamentally unsuited is, of course, only one cause of burnout. There are others. But the results of burnout, whatever its cause, are predictably the same: feeling diminished in the very qualities that characterize a personality. In other words, you lose momentarily the gift of who you are. A feeler who is under high stress, for example, becomes negative toward others. A thinker suffers a loss in achievement, orientation or ambitiousness. A sensate loses some grounding in reality. Intuitives become less enthusiastic and original. (For a thorough discussion of this point see Anna-Maria Garden, "Jungian Type, Occupation and Burnout: An Elaboration of an Earlier Study," *Journal of Psychological Type,* volume 14, 1988, pp. 2ff.)

Fourth, the shadow is where some people encounter God most deeply. For some people, God is so wholly other that to approach Him in the same way we approach the rest of life is considered obscene! They see their shadow personality somehow as the holy ground where God can be approached, while their dominant personality is secular ground where the business of life may be appropriately conducted. As one man put it, "I'm a noisy guy in a noisy environment all week. When I come before the Lord the last thing I want is a noisy, high-energy form of worship. I want to be still before the Lord." Here is another reason to learn about the shadow. Should you encounter God there, you will want to be able to make the most of this experience.

Fifth, the potential blessings of the emerging shadow can be lost through fear or through ignorance. For those whose overarching posture in life is to look good in their own and others' eyes, the tendency is to try to repress the emerging shadow: "I am going to put this source of foolishness and insecurity back in its box where it belongs!" If that happens, at best, an opportunity will be lost; at worst, it just won't work. The shadow will emerge anyway and blindside the person who thought he or she had repressed it.

For others, the emergence of the shadow is an unwelcome surprise and throws them into a tailspin. Sometimes the so-called midlife crisis is caused or made worse by the surprise emergence of, and inability to deal with, this unfamiliar side to the personality.

I once shared this information with a group of retired businessmen and to illustrate it told a story, from a composite of individuals, about the emergence of the shadow in a middle-aged businessman to whom I gave the name Trip Wharton. He is an ISTJ. Here is a brief review of what that means.

The extravert/introvert axis measures our relationship to the world around us. Trip is an introvert, preferring the world within himself to the world of people.

The sensate/intuitive axis describes where a person finds the data our minds analyze and how he or she gathers the information needed for making decisions. As a sensate, Trip is oriented toward specific detail and a literal understanding rather than speculative hunches or the symbolic.

The thinker/feeler axis shows the basis on which a person makes decisions. Trip, a thinker, tends to make his decisions on the basis of fixed principles and logical analysis rather than on the basis of emotions or personal considerations.

The judge/perceiver axis tells us a person's relative like or dislike of structure, planning, order and conclusion; Trip, being a judge, likes structure and plans rather than spontaneity. He also enjoys work over play.

I told the group of retired businessmen that Trip Wharton, as an ISTJ, had been a no-nonsense, nose-to-the-grindstone businessman whose wife, Wendy, an ENFP, was always trying to get Trip to take a cruise, enjoy (not financially appraise) works of art, and, in general, stop to smell the roses. This was not Trip, and he would not do it.

One day, in his mid-forties, Trip started noticing some strange things happening to him. He was experiencing feelings distinctly odd. He was starting to chitchat around the water cooler. His lunch hours stretched because he was stopping to watch street performers. He was noticing and admiring things of beauty. These were new things and as a result he wasn't sure what to do with them. In fact, he was somewhat embarrassed by them for they went against every way he believed a prominent businessman should behave.

One day he went home and surprised Wendy with a big hug and the announcement that he had purchased two tickets for a cruise. This was so unlike her husband that Wendy, whose playful, spontaneous personality had been crushed by Trip over the years, grew suspicious. She wondered, in fact, if this were not a guilt offering for some transgression her husband had committed! That suspicion, plus years of hurt, welled up and expressed itself in derisive laughter. Insecure as he was about this new way of acting, Trip was hurt. Wasn't he finally doing what Wendy had been after him to do for years? Hurt at home, and vulnerable to the new, untested emotions he was feeling, Trip wound up distant from his wife and involved in an affair.

When I told this story, to my astonishment, half the men in the room were wiping tears from their eyes! One of them finally spoke up. "Mark, you are describing what happened to several of us when our middle-age crisis came." After a few moments, several of them said they wished they had been aware of personality type and the emerging of various aspects of the shadow as they entered midlife. I realize fully that a stronger moral commitment could have stopped at least some of them from their adulterous flings. But as we know, the tempter is subtle and we are wise if we are aware of the various tricks he uses to try to make us fall. To be aware that the devil may use our emerging shadow to make middle age a disaster instead of a time of enrichment is one way of keeping a step ahead of him.

Some have concluded that since integrating your emerging shadow may bring breadth of personality, a deeper understanding of other people and a closer encounter with God, you should strive for balance. They argue that you should try to live on the borderline between extravert and introvert, between sensate and intuitive, and so on. While this sounds good, it is not.

For one thing, it is better to be good at those few things you are gifted at than to be mediocre at everything. In other words, if a baseball player is gifted as a shortstop, he should spend his time becoming a better shortstop, not trying to become a pitcher. As applied to personality type, if you are an extravert, it is better to learn how to be a mature extravert than to spend time trying to become half-extravert, half-introvert. Otherwise, you will wind up not very good at either.

For another thing, in trying to force yourself to become something you are not, you will possibly wound yourself emotionally. You will convince yourself that your personality is defective, and you will so force yourself to go against the grain that you will mar, not enhance, that which God gave.

For a third thing, just as a farmer waits until fruit is ripe before picking it, so you should let God ripen your personality and let the shadow emerge when it is time to. In the meantime you can learn about personality so as to respond more appropriately to situations involving other personality types. And, you can learn about the shadow side of your personality so that when it emerges you will not be blindsided.

To try to force any personality is unwise. Instead of bringing out the best of both worlds it leads only to mediocrity and confusion.

With all these thoughts about personality type in mind, let us now turn to ways in which you may have been wounded by those who did not understand or appreciate that unique person God made you to be.

3

Wounded Personalities

❖❖ In reading through the variety of personality types, perhaps you have realized how important each one is. Perhaps, too, you have put some names to these types—names of loved ones, names of acquaintances or people at work, or names of heroes of the Christian faith throughout the centuries. You might also have thought about people you know who do not allow themselves to celebrate the personalities God gave them. And maybe others came to mind who have tried, intentionally or unknowingly, to limit the rich diversity of personality types. These are the ones who have wounded other people just for being themselves. How does it happen?

Perhaps the most common way personality is wounded is to grow up where the significant figures are of a different personality. Such significant figures can be parents, siblings, teachers, close friends, leaders at church. We saw in chapter 1 how difficult it was for Gina to fit into her energetic, talkative Italian family. No one was trying to hurt Gina, but since everyone else was outgoing, they assumed Gina must be misbehaving. Since these extraverts assumed that being extravert was the normal way to be, they inadvertently ran roughshod over an introvert.

Now imagine the opposite scenario, an extravert living in an introvert family. Picture a bubbly little extravert child—let's call him Andy—in a family of quiet people. Andy's parents are loving and care deeply about him. What they do not like is the way he comes home from school. Andy bursts into the kitchen, talking nonstop about absolutely every detail of the day.

His parents try to keep up, but after about fifteen minutes of this they are utterly exhausted. Eventually they tell Andy to be quiet, one of them goes to the medicine chest for the aspirin and they spend the next few hours avoiding him until their energy levels return.

What might be the results of this on the emotions and personality? There are generally two outcomes.

It is possible that the criticism would do no harm. Some people are not troubled by reactions like these. They chalk it up to another learning experience and grow up being themselves but in a more mature way.

More likely, however, the individuals will be hurt. They may try to change, to become what they are not and lose the gift of who they are. Or they may grow hardened and less sensitive to the feelings of others. The wise counsel to be true to oneself can be twisted into be true to myself, no matter how it harms anyone else.

Let's look now at three aspects of woundedness: the internal response to criticism, how not to hurt others and how you might express the wounds you have received.

The Internal Response

Direct criticism of behavior, attitudes or outlook may cause you to believe that there is something seriously wrong with you.

Sooner or later in conversation, for instance, the Andys of this world might hear statements like: "Why are you so loud? Andy, it's O.K. to be enthusiastic, but you are draining us with your energy. Tone it down! Andy, you've been talking nonstop for ten minutes. Give somebody else a turn."

If these statements strike a nerve, Andy will go to his room thinking, *Here we go again. I come home excited about the events of the day, wanting to share them with the people I love. Look what happened. Look what always happens. I get yelled at. I get sent away. Either they don't really love me or there is something wrong with me. I can't figure it out.* Keep repeating this sort of event and before long the wound is deep. *Something wrong with me.* . . . This is a significant statement, for it reveals a shame orientation.

Shame orientation happens in a family when communication of thoughts and feelings is ignored, rejected, repudiated or not validated. Toxic shame has to do with the way you feel about yourself based upon how others have mistreated you. It is not based upon what you have done wrong. Feelings arising from what you have done wrong are the basis for guilt and appropriate, healthy shame. Toxic shame, however, is based on the responses of people who, for whatever reason, confuse matters of right and wrong with matters of personality and style. The way out of shame is not through improved performance—trying to become what others want you to be—but through receiving the good news about who you are and how God sees you. (For more information, see *Healing the Shame that Binds You* by John Bradshaw.)

The criticism Gina received was the opposite of Andy's: "Don't be so aloof! Go downstairs and talk to your family." Gina's problem would not be over if she did go downstairs. If she acted true to her introvert self and shared a few thoughts in a low-key manner, one of her extravert relatives might well respond, "What's the matter, Gina? Cat got your tongue? Talk to me."

Poor Gina. Her internal response to this recurrent scene is to think, *What's wrong with me? Why can't I carry on a conversation? Why don't I want to be with these people as much as others do? I think I love them, but I don't know. Maybe I'm not really very loving.*

Remember, according to the Myers-Briggs Type Indicator, personalities can be understood in four different ways. Let's look at three of them—sensate/intuitive, thinker/feeler and judge/perceiver—in regard to the internal response to criticism.

Sensate/intuitive personality has to do with where you find the data and how you gather the information needed for making decisions. Direct criticism of sensates and intuitives might go like this.

A sensate child (one who is good at noticing details but not the big picture, and whose mind is far more literal than imaginative) might be criticized by a teacher during story time in this manner: "Harold, you are such a dullard. Why can't you come up with a little make-believe story? Look at your classmates. They're doing a wonderful job spinning their tales. All you're doing is sitting there drawing little machine-like figures on your notepad."

A sensate in a Bible study might be put down as a literalist for wanting to focus on what the text actually says, rather than what some of the intuitives think it could have said or might conceivably mean.

The sensate might internalize this by thinking, *Maybe I am a dullard!* Over the years I have met a number of people who could well have done much better but, believing they were of limited ability, stopped trying. Let me retell briefly the story of someone like that, a story I first related in *Christian Healing*.

I know a woman, whom I'll call Irene, who struck me as

brilliant, yet held an unchallenging, low-paying job. When I told her it seemed to me a woman with her abilities could have a leadership position and a high salary, she responded that she was not good enough for anything like that. I tried to convince her that several others agreed with me but she refused to believe it.

Over a period of time, through prayer and counseling, we discovered that in junior high a teacher, who disliked Irene, had told her she was a *C* student and would probably not amount to very much. That teacher was respected and his views carried weight. Somehow the message was internalized. It was as if Irene adopted a script for life, written by this teacher. She began subconsciously to act her part, that of a *C* student who would never amount to very much. Not coincidentally, she had been an *A/B* student up until that point.

It took time, but gradually Irene gained confidence and fulfilled her God-given potential.

The intuitive is the one who can brainstorm and imagine but who has difficulty with the precise and routine.

Do you remember Paul, that mystical, creative teenager in a family of engineers we met in chapter 1? From his well-meaning parents, Paul might hear this: "There you go, sketching in your notebook and not attending to your schoolwork. Don't you know that the first thing to go in a budget cutback is the fine arts? Stop wasting your time on frivolities and prepare for a career that will put food on the table."

Or, an intuitive church committee member might be told, "Walter, you always come up with ideas but none of them squares with reality. Never mind your visions. Look at the facts!"

In response, Paul and Walter might deny their creativity. Paul might start to believe that art is frivolous and feel guilty whenever he sketches something. Walter might think to himself, *Every time I come up with an idea, they rain on my parade. No more! I'll keep my ideas to myself.* A wounded intuitive may lose the idealism that, while sometimes impractical, holds out the belief that things can be better.

Thinker/feeler personality describes the basis on which you tend to make decisions. The thinker decides on a more dispassionate scale of what is right or what follows the rules. The feeler is more prone to take into account exceptions to the rules and decide from the heart. Response to direct criticism might go like this:

A thinker might be told by her feeler friends, "Barbara, we know there is no anger in you or in your tone of voice, but you just can't go around saying what you think. You have to be aware that your opinions might hurt people's feelings. You have to be indirect in what you say, and focus on people, not ideas. People are interested in warmth, not opinions."

Or, a thinker's practical way of showing love might not be appreciated by a feeler. "Ann, I do appreciate your picking up the dry cleaning to save me an extra trip, but I'd feel more loved if you hugged me instead."

One possible response of a thinker might be to believe everything his critics are saying and deny his personality in the process. He might try to do better by being more loving *as defined by the feelers.*

A "feeling" church active in feeding the homeless might be told, "Why do you waste your time on people like that? Many of them are that way because people like you give them incentives to stay on the streets."

Or, a feeler might be told by her husband, "Claudia, you are such a bleeding heart! Those boys who keep damaging our garden need discipline from their parents, not your understanding. I've gone along with your request to do nothing long enough. You are not helping them by making excuses for them."

What might Claudia's response be? She might shrug it off. But if it wounds her, she might become unsure what to do, deferring to her husband for a response.

Or, she might react with hostility. People wonder how anyone who is hostile could truly be a feeler since feelers are supposed to have a big soft place in their hearts for others. Some would conclude that Claudia, in this case, must be a thinker.

A thinker, however, would present herself as somewhat distant from a person's inner feelings. Claudia, even in hostility, is not distant. Since her personality was wounded, or at least the feeler aspect of it, her feeler response has become twisted. So her response is still as a feeler, but as a *wounded* feeler. She is still oriented toward others, but her response has become distorted from compassion into anger.

Or, having been put down for having too much love and not enough truth, Claudia might jump to the opposite pole and call the police and press charges against the boys disturbing their garden. Subconsciously she might be thinking, *If being a feeling person is wrong, I'll just change.* It won't work, however, for Claudia to take up her shadow thinker side, for two reasons. First, she doesn't know very much about being a thinker, about how to make use of that shadow function. Second, she's not allowing it to flow naturally. She's using it as a weapon.

The issue, of course, is not the problem with the garden or helping the boys learn an appropriate lesson of life. The issue is Claudia's need for and attempt to gain some self-esteem. But self-esteem comes from God, not from trying to please others. Even if Claudia were, momentarily, to gain the approval of her critics, thinking ill of herself would take away any momentary good feelings. In addition, until her personality was healed and her self-esteem firmly anchored in her relationship with God,

Claudia would be highly susceptible to the next person who yelled at her for being herself.

As an aside, we see how the tangled web of hurt feelings can snare others. If Claudia pressed charges with the police, for instance, trying to defend her wounded self, she might poison relationships with the neighbors and embitter the boys against discipline. This example should show us that being healed is not just for our sakes, but for the sakes of all those our lives touch.

Judge/perceiver personality measures the relative like or dislike of structure, planning, order and conclusion. A judge is not necessarily one who is judgmental—don't confuse those two words—but rather a person who likes structure, plans, order and predictability. A perceiver, likewise, is not necessarily one who is more perceptive but rather a person who likes things unstructured, informal, flexible and spontaneous. How might judges and perceivers be wounded?

A responsible young man whose personality is that of a judge might be told by his perceiver friends, "George, stop being so rigid. Life is to enjoy. Loosen up! Smell the flowers."

Similarly, a judge on a church committee might feel pressure to stop pushing the group to plan for the coming year: "Bill, let the Holy Spirit work it out. Don't you know that human planning just gets in the way of God?"

In response, the judge might overreact and conclude that *any* sense of duty, not just an overdeveloped one, is wrong. In reaction, he may turn into a Peter Pan, a childish, irresponsible adult who never grows up. In church, the wounded judge might conclude that if planning *could* get in the way of the Holy Spirit, all planning *does* get in the way, and, since we don't want to be disrespectful to God, maybe we shouldn't plan anything anymore. In terms of worship, any preplanned order of service may gradually be looked at with suspicion.

A young perceiver might be told by his judge mother, "Donald, when I tell you to get your chores done, I mean right now! Work first, then play. I realize you get them done eventually, but in the meantime I have to look at the disorder in this house. Stop being a goof-off and finish your work."

Rachel, a perceiver on a committee, might find other committee members unsympathetic with her desire to wait until they can examine the problem from other angles.

If Rachel is wounded by this criticism, she might try to make a decision more quickly. Unfortunately, not being used to this, the unfortunate perceiver often picks the wrong occasion to rush it. Or, Donald and Rachel might be so eager to do the "right" thing—getting the chores done, coming to a conclusion, making a decision—that they become immobilized, just the opposite of what they and their critics desire.

We have been looking at the chief way emotions can be wounded—when the significant figures in an individual's life fail to understand or honor his or her personality type. In this instance we examined how the direct criticism of our behavior, attitudes or outlook may lead us to believe that there is something seriously wrong with us.

We will look in a moment at some of the ways we express this woundedness, perhaps seeing ourselves. But I want to take a moment here to point out that if you are someone's role model, parent, teacher, and you have a different personality type, you can avoid passing on this woundedness to others. Here's how.

Free Expression

While acknowledging that in some cases even the most carefully chosen words will wound the overly sensitive, we can try to communicate love and acceptance at the heart of any negative comments. We can learn to change criticism into communication.

One of the best examples I can think of came from an introvert friend of mine. He said to me, "Mark, one of the things I love about you is your zest for life. You enjoy things to the max, and share your enthusiasm with others. It's great. But I'm a quiet soul. It would help me if you could share in a gentler way. That way I can receive the gift of your conversation even better. I'm not saying there's anything wrong with you, or with me. It's just that the bridge between the two of us needs to be relocated a bit so the traffic can flow better. O.K.?"

We can further help others not be bound by allowing them, or helping them find, an appropriate forum for expression. Most of us can accept the fact that the expression of personality should not come at the expense of the needs and rights of others. But if there is never a time or way to express who we are, sooner or later we start to feel rejected. If Andy only ever heard, "You've talked enough, Andy, give somebody else a turn," and was never given another chance until, once again, he bubbled over on his own accord, he might start to feel that nobody was interested.

Suppose Andy's parents approached their situation this way. After one of his initial rapid-fire reports, they might say, "Andy, we want to hear more, but we need to do something else right now. Right after we watch the news tonight, let's talk more about your day." Andy would believe that his parents cared about him and were looking forward to his sharing.

What could Gina's boisterous parents do to soften any possible wounding of their quiet daughter? If they came to realize that Gina acts the way she does because she is an introvert, not aloof or rude, they might say something like this:

"Gina, we recognize that this high-energy family drains you. Why don't we try this: When company comes, make the rounds for a half hour or so. Then you can go to your room and be by yourself. We'll cover for you. After a while, rejoin us for as long as you can. Most of our relatives remember Uncle Salvatore from the old country. He was quiet like you. We'll explain that you are like him and that they need to be less energetic with you. Those who don't understand, well, we'll try to be a buffer for you." I know a family that tried this with great success.

Harold, the dullard, could be turned into Harold, the boy of a thousand clues, during story time if his sensate gift were recognized and utilized. Harold's teacher, noting his gift for observation and detail, might assign him the task of putting the details into the creative stories of others. If a classmate told a story about the search for an elusive porcupine, Harold might be given the task of describing in detail the pizza factory in which the porcupine hid, and the Dick Tracy outfit the junior detective wore. Intuitives, gifted at the big picture, would value Harold's detail work. Harold, in turn, would have his chance to shine.

The sensates in a Bible study might be thanked for keeping the intuitives from going so far into interpretation that they begin speculating far beyond what God has revealed in Scripture. In one Bible study I attended, Charlie, a strong sensate, was called the anchor because whenever people started floating away into flights of speculation, Charlie would always keep them anchored in the text.

Paul, the creative, artistic intuitive, might be told, "It's a good thing to have a few skills to fall back on, just in case. We don't understand your artistic work, but people who know these things tell us you are quite good at it. We'd like to affirm that. Here's the deal. We'll encourage and pay for your art lessons if you agree also to study something, shall we say, more practical. And, yes, we'll go to that art exhibit with you. You may have to

Free to Be Me!

explain it all to us several times before we get the point, but let's give it a try."

Walter might be told by the committee's sensate members, "While not all ideas or visions should be acted upon, we know that God is the God of the impossible. We will continue to weigh the visions you come up with. We will probably be able to act on only a few of them but, Walter, keep at it. We would never think of these things ourselves."

Barbara, the thinker, might start to believe that she is unloving, since she does not show warmth and sympathy like her feeler friends and seems to offend them with her honest opinions. If they were as warm toward Barbara as they want her to be toward others, they would find opportunities to praise her more objective stance. They might realize that sometimes they get taken in by a sob story. They could ask Barbara to cut through the fog of emotions to get to the facts. And when Barbara does save the day, they could praise her for her valuable contribution.

"Thanks, Babs. We supply the heat, but you supply the light. We sure do need each other."

Ann might be told by her husband, "I know that when you do these practical things for me, like going to the dry cleaner to save me a trip, it is expressive of love. I'm learning to recognize and receive love offered this way." At the same time, Ann might learn how to show her love in a more emotional, feeling way, too.

The "bleeding-heart" Claudia, who seems to have an extra measure of compassion, might be encouraged to express it by volunteering in the hospital or working in a soup kitchen. By allowing her personality to be expressed and valued, Claudia can then learn when a more objective response is appropriate.

The church, so active in its works of compassion, would first need to be commended for its extra mile of loving activity before being warned about "enabling" some of its soup kitchen guests. I once heard a loving church admonished this way: "What you're doing here at St. Andrew's is incredible. I've never seen a church where the members pitched in more actively to help the underprivileged in such a practical way. Remember, though, that some people need 'tough love' in order to develop more responsible behavior. I've had some experience in this and would like to share what I've learned about how we can help those truly down on their luck without reinforcing the irresponsible behavior of the minority who are abusing your love."

George, the judge, might find that his friends' lackadaisical approach to life keeps them from having the kind of fun that can come with planning. They would like to go horseback riding, but that would involve calling different stables and making arrangements. That's too much work, so they settle for a game of kick-the-can.

But when they realize that George thrives on structure, planning and order, they can ask him to do the arranging. George is given a way to express who he is. The result? His friends appreciate what he does for them, George feels good about himself and the stable owner gets some extra business.

Perceiver Donald, who gets things done eventually, might be given an opportunity to get to his mother's goal line but via his own circuitous route. His mother might say, "Here are several things that you need to do. They must be done within a week. How you do them and when is up to you. You can get them done immediately, or eventually, and in any order you choose. We know you like to do things according to your own plan (or, ahem, lack of plan), so here's your chance."

In short, there are ways to affirm a person's personality while not necessarily accepting the particular thought or action of the moment. Whether in correcting something inappropriate or in saying we think a different approach is called for in this circumstance, we are telling people that we love them and that their personality types are valued.

(We need to add parenthetically, although it is beyond the scope of this book, that another way personality can be wounded is by growing up in a home where self-esteem is shattered through various forms of abuse. When a personality is wounded to this degree, the kinds of responses suggested in this book might not work. *Any* suggestion of a different approach is heard as rejection, no matter how lovingly given. In those cases I recommend, in addition to prayer for inner healing, in-depth Christian therapy by those specially gifted and trained.)

It may not be too late for others, but suppose the damage has been done. Do you wonder if you have been wounded? Perhaps you are sure of it. Read the expressions of woundedness given below and see if you find yourself in any of these. We will be exploring healing in the chapters that follow.

The Expressions of Hurt

If you have been wounded, the expression of that hurt will come out in one of several ways.

First, as a wounded person you may try to be the opposite of who you are. Instead of staying true to yourself while learning to be sensitive in your relationships with others, you might find yourself trying to become what others have pressured you to be.

"That's what they want, isn't it?" a wounded extravert once told me. "They're always after me to be quiet. I guess that's what I'll have to be if I want to get along." This man has, to a greater or lesser degree, bought into the lie that certain personalities are better than others. He has concluded that his personality must be faulty—after all, it seems to engender negative comments—and that another personality might be more virtuous.

Few people can actually pull off being something they're not. As an illustration of this, try writing your name with your opposite hand. For many this isn't especially hard, although the signature may look like the handwriting of a second-grader. In fact, writing with the opposite hand for a few moments is often fun. But try writing that way for an hour! It quickly becomes quite tedious.

I once asked a group of people to write with their opposite hand. I told them to keep writing until I told them to stop and that this might not be for quite some time. After about ten minutes one man slammed down his pen and said, "If God wanted me to write with my left hand, He would have made me a southpaw in the first place! I quit!"

It is the same with trying to be a personality you are not made to be. You can pull it off for a while but will soon become exhausted with the effort; it is unnatural.

Carl realized that he, a thinker, should summon up as much feeler in him as was possible when around his Aunt Cassie. His feeler expressions of love were genuine, for Carl did care for his aunt, and he could maintain it for a while. But when he tried to adopt the feeler mode in relating to everyone, it came off as ingratiating, as hollow and insincere. He had enough emotional energy to summon up his feeler side when needed, but not enough to pull it off on a consistent basis.

He was in a double bind. He had been told that being a thinker wasn't good enough. But when he tried to be a feeler he was accused of being phony. Carl couldn't win no matter what he tried. He accepted the lie that expressing a different personality was better, yet he had no rewards to show for it. He was left exhausted and confused. He alternated between putting down other thinkers for being uncaring and feelers for being insincere.

Free to Be Me!

This is a classic victim-becomes-victimizer pattern. In fact, more than a few of the people who so harshly put down the personalities of others were themselves put down as youngsters.

If you have been frustrated in summoning the shadow side of your personality for an incorrect reason (to act in a way that will finally let you feel good about yourself and be accepted by others), you may shy away from trying to summon it when it would be appropriate.

In extreme cases, when there is also physical trauma, sexual abuse or other major, long-lasting distress, the personality may actually split as a defense mechanism. This can lead to multiple personality disorders and other serious complications.

Second, as a wounded person you may just give up. It is exhausting to keep up the effort to be something you are not. Eventually you give up. Any effort in self-improvement is, you conclude, futile. Scriptural promises that you can, by God's grace, become a holier person are dismissed as pious platitudes. Testimonies of others are dismissed as delusions. You conclude that you are just not a first-class person. You shut down emotionally. John and Paula Sandford use the term *slumbering spirit* to describe the soul of a person who has given up. Unless something breaks into this cycle of failure and despair, you will never find happiness.

Third, you may get angry and not care about appropriate behavior. Nancy, a thinker, grew up with parents who were feelers. Her church placed great emphasis on sharing one's love in emotional and tactile ways. This wasn't Nancy! They kept telling her that they did not perceive her as particularly loving. Nancy thought she was, although she found it difficult to express in emotional ways.

"I like to express my love for people by helping them in practical ways," she said. "I care for people as much as anyone else, but I'm not the huggy type. I'd much rather find specific needs people have and work to meet them."

Although this may make sense to you and me, it did not particularly register with her parents or her church. For a while Nancy tried to meet them halfway. She tried expressing her love more emotionally. She tried hugging, for instance, during the "exchange of the peace" at church.

"But nobody met *me* halfway," Nancy lamented. "They saw my efforts not as the attempt at bridging different personalities, but as me starting to learn how to be loving. I've tried but I'm tired of being the only one who has to try. I've had enough! From now on I'm going to love on my terms. If people can't handle this, that's just too bad."

I expressed my concern for Nancy and told her I thought others were not being sensitive to her. I encouraged her not to stop trying to construct bridges to others, even though it seemed they were not doing their share of the building. But nothing I told her made any difference. As a result, Nancy lost out on what could have been a number of good friendships, and, in her anger, wound up wounding the personalities of others, just as she had been wounded. Angry people may bottle up their anger, becoming depressed in the process. Or they may indulge in passive-aggressive behavior, using a quiet and gentle surface demeanor to mask a hostile undermining of others.

Or they may express such anger directly by becoming critical of everybody and everything. They take negative comments personally. Intuitives, particularly, have some emotional investment in their ideas and, when wounded, they may take disagreement with their ideas as a personal attack.

We are witnessing in the Church several groups who want their views or lifestyles accepted within the mainstream. Often their response to those who disagree with them, however lovingly or gently, is anger. "You are rejecting me," one person said to me when I expressed mild disagreement with something he had said. Some go even further and say that since Christians must love other people we must agree with their views or behaviors, no matter how different. If that were the case, Jesus would not qualify! Such expressions of anger are symptomatic, in fact, of the need for major healing. The most loving thing the Church can do is to stick to the truth that God has given us once for all in Scripture and minister that truth lovingly but unwaveringly to all.

We must compassionately and firmly correct those who insist on lashing out at others because of their own woundedness. Otherwise, the cycle will continue. When I hear a wounded woman attempt to justify her rudeness toward men by telling me how men have mistreated her, I try to point out that all she is doing is giving those men an excuse to seek their own revenge against other women. When will the cycle end? The answer is, when people forgive.

What a tragedy it is when people live their entire lives with wounded personalities. It is especially tragic because this does not have to happen. Our help comes in realizing that woundedness can be healed. In the next chapter I outline some ways to receive healing for wounded personalities. In following chapters I want to describe some ways we can celebrate the richness of diversity that God has given to us all.

4

Healing Your Wounded Personality

❖ Now that we have looked at how personalities are wounded, let's look at how they may be healed.

Although some individuals may need long-term professional care, most people do not require such intensive or expensive treatment. I wish to describe in this chapter a process of healing that you can use for yourself and others. This process is known as inner healing, or emotional healing. David Seamands refers to it as healing for damaged emotions.

I am going to walk you through the basic steps involved in inner healing, applying it specifically to wounded personalities. If you would like to go deeper into the process of inner healing, consult the bibliography at the end of this book for a sampling of the many excellent books on the subject.

The first step toward healing your wounded personality is to acknowledge that your personality is a gift to you from God Himself. And as Ethel Waters so wonderfully put it, "God don't make junk."

At first this may be difficult for you to believe. You are doubtless aware of what you do wrong. The unloving words of those not affirming your personality may ring in your ears. Yes, you must repent of your sins. Yes, you need to cooperate with God to grow into maturity. But the fact remains: God gave you your personality as a gift. You may need to remind yourself of this truth many times a day because you have heard hundreds, perhaps thousands, of statements to the contrary. These won't usually evaporate with just a few words of affirmation.

Neither will they evaporate with words of affirmation that are self-generated. Unless affirmation comes from outside—from God and from others—it will mean little. All the slogans and self-help books in the world will not get a person who denigrates him or herself to think otherwise. I met a man who tried. He went around reciting self-affirming slogans to himself for a few weeks and then shared this with me: "I don't believe those slogans. They were written by a jerk who doesn't know what he's talking about—*me!*" Real affirmation has to come from outside.

Some people have found it helpful to write down on 3 x 5 cards statements of biblical truth, such as:

My personality is God's gift to me.

I am made in the image of God.

God loves me very much.

Others take a scriptural promise and personalize it. For example:

God loves [your name] so much that He gave His only begotten Son, so that if [your name] believes in Him, [your name] will not perish, but have everlasting life (John 3:16).

> If [your name] is in Christ, [your name] is a new creation. The old has gone, the new has come (2 Corinthians 5:17)!

> "I have come that [your name] might have life and have it more abundantly" (John 10:10).

You may wish to put these cards in prominent places around the house or carry them in your pocket and refer to them several times a day.

Some object to this procedure, saying that it sounds like secular self-help philosophy. To be sure, there are those who have placed such statements in a context that denies the reality of sin, the need for God's grace and the necessity for growth in holiness. I am not talking about that. I am talking about affirming the truths God has promised you in Scripture, statements that are true, and true *for you,* no matter how self-deprecating your thinking or how bad you may feel at the moment.

In seeking to acknowledge that your personality is a gift from God, it is most helpful to seek relationships that will affirm that fact. Affirming relationships are vitally important! You may know intellectually about the unconditional love of God, but there is nothing like being loved unconditionally by other people to illustrate that truth and communicate it to us. We will look at ways that loving, affirming relationships can help us become whole in the final three chapters of this book.

These affirming relationships reinforce a basic truth, that *God wishes to transform you, not destroy you.* As a favorite old hymn puts it, His desire is "thy dross to consume, and thy gold to refine."

In other words, yes, of course, after you have put your trust in Christ as Lord and Savior, there is still work needed (thy dross to

Free to Be Me!

consume). But that work is to make you a better version of who you are, so the gold—the personality God gave you at your conception—can shine. After conversion (whether dramatic or quiet, sudden or gradual) it is the work of the Holy Spirit to bring sanctification. His job is to make you whole, and this is a word of rich, full meaning. It says that not only does God want you to be holy, He also wants you to enjoy *wholeness*. That includes a healthy expression of personality.

Until you accept the fact that God wants to develop in you a better version of your personality, not swap it for a different one, the rest of the steps in the inner healing process that follow will not work. Until you believe this, you will not cooperate with God's process of healing because you are likely convinced that God will not "waste His time on people like me." Or you will exhaust yourself trying to be someone you are not, and waste the valuable energy needed to become a better version of who you really are.

I remember when I was in college trying to do that. I was very aware of how my being an extravert got me into trouble. It seemed as if I was always saying the wrong thing and hurting others and embarrassing myself. Some of my friends told me I did not know how to act. I concluded that since being outgoing always got me into trouble, I had better do some changing. One night I went to bed vowing that the next morning I would be shy. It didn't work, of course. All that happened was that I got worse! I could pull off keeping things in for only so long. Then, exhausted from trying to be someone I wasn't, out came the old Mark, usually in a worse manner than before.

This continued for some time until a wise old priest, after chewing me out for something I had just said, stopped, took me by the hand, looked at me directly and said, "But, Mark, don't ever change!"

I said to him, "I'm confused! You've just told me that my style of relating is wrong. Now you're telling me not to change. Which is it?"

He said that I wasn't in trouble because I was an extravert. He told me, "Being an extravert just determines *how* you get into trouble. We introverts get into trouble in relating to people, too, but in a different way. What you need is to learn how to be a better extravert, not stop being one. It's O.K. to be you, but what you need is to be a better version of that, and it can't start until you finally accept the fact that God made you an extravert, and that's O.K."

Once I stopped trying to change myself and cooperated with what God was trying to do, I discovered that things improved considerably.

It is very important at this juncture to state that we should *never* take this attitude—"God made me this way, so it's O.K. to be me"—when sin is involved. In other words it is never correct to say, "I'm a racist [or greedy person or misogynist or adulterer or sexual pervert] because God made me that way. The Church must accept me for what I am and help me thank God for this orientation."

God has shown in Scripture both the breadth and the limits of "inclusivity": inclusive of all kinds of personality types, of both sexes, of various levels of education, income, nationality and so on; inclusive in terms of love of all people (Galatians 3:26-28). But *not* inclusive in terms of doctrine, spiritual practice and morals condemned by Scripture (Ephesians 5:3-14).

The God who gave these commands to the human race certainly knows that in a fallen world there are many reasons why we may sin. But while God understands these reasons, and loves us unconditionally, that does not mean He condones sin. Whether our various predispositions to act in certain ways contrary to

Free to Be Me!

God's will stem from choices we make freely, from being raised in an abusive home or even from having damaged DNA, God expects us to obey His commandments. The all-wise God took into account all the possible reasons why people may be predisposed to being, thinking or acting a certain way when He gave His commandments, *and gave them nonetheless.*

The second step in your healing is to ask Jesus to heal you of whatever damage may have been done to your personality. This damage occurs at various levels. Let me put it this way: There is damage at the level of *roots* and at the level of *fruits*. *Roots* mean the core of who you are. *Fruits* mean the ways you think, feel and relate as a result.

Healing at the level of roots can take longer than healing at the level of fruits. God will occasionally heal someone in an instant at both levels. God will sometimes heal the root woundedness in an instant, but help you through a whole new process of thinking, feeling and relating, since the old ways were based on a lie. More likely, He will heal both the roots and the fruits gradually.

How do you ask Jesus to heal your wounded personality? There are two ways. First, go regularly to the Lord and ask Him to help you appreciate the personality He gave you and heal both the root problem and any present-day consequences. You might offer a simple prayer like this: "Lord Jesus, please help me to accept the person that You made me to be. Please heal the woundedness in my personality done to me by others, and help me to grow in maturity. Amen." A simple prayer from the heart, offered to God on a regular basis, will do wonders.

Second, offer to God specific moments of the past and present where it is obvious your personality still needs healing.

As for the past, ask God to cleanse those painful recollections of words that put down your personality. Sometimes those memories are very clear. A woman once told me that scarcely a day

Healing Your Wounded Personality

went by that she didn't remember how her father used to ridicule her for her deep compassion toward people and animals in distress. My response was that whenever those painful recollections came to mind she should offer a simple prayer asking God to take away the emotional hurt. If she did that, eventually the pain would go away; and it did.

Sometimes you may not be aware of a memory until something triggers it. In other words, you are vaguely aware that you were put down for being yourself, but cannot recollect specific instances.

A man, Arthur by name, who is much more the flexible perceiver than structured judge, once shared with me how he became aware of his need of healing. He heard me say that often our fears and prejudices that seem on the surface to be irrational stem from painful events in the past that have been repressed into the subconscious mind. The seemingly inexplicable reaction we have to certain sights, smells, sounds, kinds of persons, objects and the like, often are clues pointing us to something deeper, something that needs to be healed.

For Arthur, the sight of an American flag triggered strongly negative feelings. "Whenever I see an American flag," he said when he came for a session of healing, "I feel very insecure about myself." He knew it wasn't because he hated America, or even strongly disagreed with what our leaders were doing. He knew it had to be something else.

We talked at some length about painful events in his life in which an American flag played a part. He asked family members if they had any ideas. We found out finally the source of the problem.

Arthur once had a summer job at a company that kept a beautifully landscaped lawn, in the middle of which was a flagpole. Part of his job was to raise and lower the flag at the beginning and

Free to Be Me!

end of the work day. One summer there was a change of bosses. His old boss had not minded if the flag was raised or lowered a few minutes late or early, a lack of precision which suited Arthur's temperament fine. The new boss, however, was a stickler for precision. The flag had to be up at eight A.M. and down at five P.M., period! Arthur failed to see the urgency in such hyper-punctuality and his boss interpreted Arthur's more casual style as loafing. All that summer the boss took it on himself, as his personal project, to whip that boy into shape. Instead of making Arthur more punctual, all it did was wound him emotionally.

For years Arthur had wondered why the sight of the American flag had such a negative effect on him. Now he knew. I suggested that whenever Arthur saw an American flag and started to experience those negative feelings about himself, he offer a prayer for the Lord to heal him of those feelings.

Sometimes just becoming aware of the events of the past that caused us pain and offering those to the Lord in prayer is sufficient for a healing to occur. Sometimes, however, the hurts still remain. In these cases I have found it a helpful procedure to picture, with the help of the Holy Spirit, the past events with Jesus in them.

I asked Arthur, for instance, to describe for me one of the occasions when his boss chewed him out for raising the flag ten minutes late. I then told Arthur to picture Jesus standing next to him, telling him that while he needed to raise the flag when the boss told him to—he was, after all, the boss—Arthur was loved and cherished for who he was. I then asked Arthur if he wanted to talk to Jesus about what he was feeling at the moment, and he did. Right there in my office Arthur poured out to Jesus the hurts and feelings of worthlessness that he had kept bottled up for years. It was the beginning of Arthur's healing.

It is important in using such an exercise to make sure that it is based strictly on the truths of Scripture. It is scriptural to picture Jesus standing with us because of His promise to be with us always, even unto the end of the age. It is scriptural to hear Jesus utter affirming words about us because the Bible tells us God loves us. And it is scriptural to pour out our grief to Him because we have been encouraged to cast our cares on Him who cares for us (1 Peter 5:7). What this little exercise does is simply to take the same truths that could be expressed in doctrinal form (Jesus is always with us; Jesus loves us very much; Jesus wants to heal our hurts) and express them in story form.

It is simply a different approach to the memory. Those familiar with the concept of "left brain/right brain" will understand the doctrinal, cognitive and rational as a left-brain approach and the story form, affective and mystical as a right-brain approach.

We see Jesus making use of this right-brain way of relating in order to effect an inner healing in Peter. Peter had denied knowing Jesus three different times while warming himself by a charcoal fire during Jesus' trial (John 18:18). After Jesus' resurrection from the dead, the Lord wanted to restore Peter to fellowship. Jesus knew how terrible Peter must have felt and wanted Peter to know that everything was forgiven. Had Jesus simply told Peter he was forgiven, it might not have been enough. *Relationally,* Peter would have been restored to fellowship with Jesus. *Intellectually,* Peter would know he was forgiven. But would he feel it? Would he know it deep down? Would he know it *emotionally*?

The way Jesus reached Peter's emotions shows us that He knew about the power of the senses centuries ago. He understood what we are learning scientifically about how the mind works. We know now, for instance, that what goes on in the background, the various things our five senses pick up, get encoded chemically in our minds, all wrapped up with the emotions of the moment. This is why a certain sight, sound or smell will trigger

Free to Be Me!

various feelings in ways that often surprise us. (For years I wondered why I always felt warm and happy when I ate a root beer popsicle until I realized how, when I was young, my grandfather would let me run errands with him, always making the drugstore—and root beer popsicles—our final stop. My mind encoded the taste of root beer popsicles with the special feelings I had when I was with my grandfather.)

Peter needed to feel forgiven, and Jesus "rescued" the impression of charcoal fires for Peter by getting their sight, sound and smell associated with positive feelings, not feelings of shame and unworthiness. He knew that Peter would spend many hours in front of charcoal fires in the ensuing years. If they triggered negative feelings within Peter—something we know might well have happened—Peter's ministry would be hampered and his joy tempered. So Jesus didn't just forgive Peter; He forgave him one morning by a charcoal fire. Jesus didn't just forgive Peter; He gave Peter three chances to affirm his love for the Lord—one affirmation per previous denial (see John 21:9–19).

Some people have expressed concern that picturing Jesus in a previous event is a New Age or occultic exercise. If you were to picture an imaginary friend or some other spiritual being other than Jesus, or call out to anyone else for help, you would be in danger of opening yourself to demonic influence. If you were to believe that you could alter past events by picturing them to be the way you wished they had happened, or call out to spiritual powers to inflict harm on the one who hurt or embarrassed you, you would be indulging in magic, not Christian ministry.

But if you are not inventing truth or trying to make God be or do something contrary to how Scripture reveals Him, you are doing nothing wrong. In fact, you are doing nothing more than what Jesus did when He told His parables. Bathed in prayer, such an exercise can be very helpful whenever you become aware of hurts from the past.

It may be necessary to repeat this exercise with a number of similar events until their recollection no longer brings pain or influences your thoughts, feelings and behaviors today. We knew Arthur was healed when the sight of an American flag no longer distressed him.

You can also turn to prayer when you become aware of how hurts of the past are influencing your behavior today.

Tom loved people deeply, but because his feeler personality type was wounded in childhood he did not always express his love for people in a way that was obvious. Tom took that problem to God. "Lord God," Tom prayed, "because my feelings for others were put down as a child, I don't know how to express them. Sometimes I seem to deny them and come off as cold. Other times I overdo them and come off as insincere. Please help me express who I am in a better way."

Tom wisely did not try to become someone else, nor did he punish himself, nor did he give up, nor did he conclude that if others had a problem with him they would just have to put up with it. Tom took the matter to God, asking for His grace to grow. Tom expressed wisdom and balance when he told me, "What I want is to be true to myself and appropriate to others."

Louise was a meticulous housekeeper, sometimes to the point of irritating her family. This suggested to Louise's friend Tina that something was wrong. Louise was a happy-go-lucky, informal kind of person in everything else and because this was so out of character Tina wondered if something in Louise's past was affecting her in this area. Sure enough, Louise's mother raised Louise to believe that unless she were a neat and orderly housekeeper she would never get or keep a husband.

God's grace is both necessary and helpful for such efforts at growth. Growth is hard work, and we need God's empowering for it. But growth also leaves us vulnerable to further put-downs.

You know what it is like to try anything new. Your true friends will cheer you on and understand the trial-and-error nature of growth, but others may not be so kind. A friend of mine once decided to learn how to play the violin. Someone overheard her practicing and commented that the music sounded more like a cat in distress. My friend, very sensitive to the comments of others, put the violin away and never touched it again. We need God's grace to insulate us from the insensitive comments of others and to remind us of how He views us. Yes, the process of becoming a more whole person is risky. But the alternative of remaining wounded is worse. Go to God in prayer for His empowering help and His affirming love.

A third step in healing your wounded personality is to share your hurts with a trusted, caring friend. This friend should be mature, discreet and wise. He or she should be close enough to care yet detached enough to offer objective guidance. He or she should allow you to get the hurts out without rushing in to offer quick advice or simplistic solutions. This friend does not have to be specially trained, just loving, caring and sensitive.

A good friend can help in at least three ways. The first is simply by allowing you to get the problem out into the open. Often the power of a problem diminishes as you get it out onto the table. You see it from a different direction. You discover that the sky did not fall down because you told it. You find yourself unburdened. By listening to your story and by praying with you, a friend can help bring to the light the dark secrets that have kept you in bondage.

The second way a friend can help you is by reflecting with you on both your woundedness and healing. You learn that your woundedness, while real, does not make you either an ogre or a freak. Many others have been wounded and think, feel and act oddly at times because of it. Many others, too, are becoming whole. By placing your story in the context of the human story, a friend can help give hope.

The third way is by serving as a coach in your God-assisted efforts in growth. Your friend can give guidance as to how to live in the reality of being whole. Often your patterns of thinking, feeling and acting are ingrained. Just because you no longer have to live a certain way does not mean you won't. You need someone to guide you into new ways of being and allow you the freedom to try out these new ways without ridicule. By giving you that safe place in which to try out your new way of being, a friend can help you gain confidence in this new, more whole way that God is giving you.

Martin was in need of such a friend. Martin was raised by fastidiously neat parents who demanded he be the same. "Even my name reflects that," he told me. "Never Marty. Always Martin." Everything neatly arranged—toys, room, hair. It became clear that this wasn't just a case of a typically messy little boy and parents who wanted the house kept tidy. This was a case of a typically messy little boy and neat freaks.

It turned out that I had the opportunity to be Martin's special friend as he strove to explore the risky path toward health. Martin needed a number of things from me. First, he needed to know that it was O.K. to be somewhat untidy. God would not punish him for some dishes left out or a pile of papers in the corner. His real friends would not love him any less for being himself.

Second, he needed to learn how to accept himself and express that, but in a way that was appropriate. It did not make him a bad person to have a sloppy desk at work, but he had to learn how to handle the times when being himself clashed with the policy of the company.

My ministry to him was several-fold: I allowed him to try out different styles of personality so he could discern what was really his and what was someone else's programming. Once he decided what his real personality was, I allowed him to try it out. That way, he could both learn what were appropriate expressions of it and become comfortable with this new way of being. My hope was to provide for him a safe place for his new beginnings. He could try things out in safety. Any negative feedback was given in ways that affirmed and encouraged, not in ways that ridiculed or wounded.

The fourth step in healing your wounded personality is to ask God's forgiveness and make sure that you have forgiven yourself. It may be that you committed sin in those events in which you were wounded.

Remember Gina, the introvert in the extravert family? Perhaps Gina was rude when her mother asked her to go downstairs; or perhaps, by her behavior, it was apparent to her family that Gina did not want to be with them. In comparison to the harm unwittingly done to poor Gina, her smart remarks or grumpy disposition might not have been that bad, but God calls us to something better. His love for us is not expressed by overlooking our failures, but by calling them to our attention and forgiving us when we repent.

It is even more urgent to seek God's presence if you have a vague, undefined but quite real sense of guilt. This happens often when a person was seriously victimized, whether sexually, emotionally or both. "I must have done something terrible to deserve what happened to me" is the standard conclusion most victims reach. It may be helpful to learn through therapy or counseling that this was not the case. A person is abused because *the abuser* is acting horribly, *not the victim.* Convincing yourself—or someone else—of this truth may take time.

I have found it helpful to pray with a deeply wounded person in this way: "Dear Lord, we know that Mike responded badly when his parents acted the way they did. He asks Your forgiveness for those thoughts, words and deeds. But if there are also other sins of which he is unaware, connected with the way his parents raised him, we ask You to bring them to mind. We know You do not want us tying ourselves up in knots, forever searching our memories for everything we did wrong, so if Mike needs to know something specifically, please bring it to mind. Otherwise, we ask You to forgive those sins that will remain unknown." Prayer like that with assurance of God's pardon helps break the cycle of a victim's being revictimized with real or false guilt.

The fifth step on the path toward the healing of your personality is to forgive those who wounded you. The response to an abuser is often one of hate. If this is true of you, while it is understandable, it is a sin and something you must move past.

Jesus told us to forgive our enemies and those who have used us. This does not mean you have to like them. It certainly does not mean you have to allow them to hurt you further. But you do have to let go of the bitterness. Without such forgiveness you are kept in bondage.

This bondage is spiritual, emotional and physical. Spiritual, because the Bible says that anyone who does not forgive others will not be forgiven by God. Emotional, because negative feelings toward others can trap you in a lifestyle of bitterness and keep you from enjoying inner peace and joy. Physical, because bitterness often partially suppresses the immune system, leaving you vulnerable to all sorts of diseases.

The fact is, you will not be able to become the new person you want to be unless you let go of any bitterness you have toward the

Free to Be Me!

person or persons who wounded you. This is true whether their wounding was a deliberate attempt to cause you harm or the misguided actions of those who loved you very much. Hating, even hating abusers, is a sin.

As a Episcopal priest I hear some people applauding proposed liturgies that sit loosely on matters of sin, repentance, God's judgment, the necessity of God's grace for our growth and the like. "I want to be free from all of that restrictive nonsense," a man told me recently. "I want to go to church to be told how good I am and how I can hold my head up high. I don't want any more of this right-wing repression." I tried to point out that biblical truth is not right-wing repression but, in fact, what liberates us from repression, whatever its source. Like Lady Macbeth's perpetual handwashing, no amount of pumping oneself up with "I'm O.K." will take away the toxicity of unrepented sin.

Others want to remove language about sin from the liturgy because it excludes, or, to use the current favorite word, it marginalizes people. Yet not to tell a person about his or her sin as Scripture defines it is a worse marginalization; for until a person repents of sin, that person is estranged, not from God's love, but from fellowship with God and all the blessings that brings.

But how do you forgive? How can you control your feelings? The answer is, you cannot control your feelings, but you can control your actions. Forgiveness is, first and foremost, a decision of the will. Only secondarily is forgiveness a feeling. When you act in obedience to God and choose to forgive, after a while the feelings of forgiveness will come.

Here are two actions of forgiveness.

First, banish any thoughts of hatred or bitterness toward those who harmed you. As soon as those thoughts come into your mind, you have a choice. You can entertain them or you can tell them to go away, refusing to dwell on them. You can enjoy thinking how something dreadful might happen to your abusers, or you can pray that God will cleanse your thoughts.

Second, pray positively for those who wounded you. The key word here is *positively*. If you are like me, the effort to obey the scriptural command to pray for those who have hurt you winds up as self-righteous suggestions that these people smarten up! While they may certainly need to do so, this type of prayer is to hold a position of superiority, albeit subtly, over them. That is hardly the attitude needed to let go of bitterness. Let others pray that they are changed. Your task is to pray for them to be blessed.

I have always found it difficult to pray positively for people who hurt me. I argue, "But they don't deserve to be blessed. Look what they did to me!" When I say that, God reminds me that He sent Christ to die for my sins while I was still a sinner (Romans 5:8), so who do I think I am to say that others do not deserve blessings! I remember the effort to forgive a man who had done me wrong. It was hard to pray, "Lord, please bless him today. May Your shower of blessings fall down upon him. May he know great joy." My heart was not in it but I continued to pray positively for him for about three weeks before I started to feel forgiveness toward him. I knew that I had forgiven him when I heard someone mention his name later on and I no longer felt the bitterness.

It may be easier to forgive people who have hurt you when you remember that many of those who wound the personalities of others have had their personalities wounded themselves. This does not excuse their wrong behavior, but it does make it understandable.

For a helpful ten-step procedure to release anger, pain and judgment, see Appendix 1 in the back of this book. Some helpful suggestions on forgiveness can also be found in Phoebe Cranor's book *Five Loaves and Two Fishes*.

Free to Be Me!

The sixth step is to rewrite the old scripts that were based on lies with scripts that are based on the truth. Some use the imagery of tapes instead of the imagery of scripts.

A friend of mine, Father Lindsay Warren, has told me of a time when he found himself downcast at not being offered a position for which he had applied. Lindsay noted this was not just a normal disappointment, but one that lingered and seemed to influence everything else in his life. Praying with a friend, he was able to recall an event that happened when he was four years old. Lindsay had been sent to the store to buy a loaf of whole wheat bread. Not only did Lindsay get distracted and come home very late, he brought home white bread instead. His father was furious. In response, his father denied him a treat that Lindsay had wanted. Not only did Lindsay conclude *I am a bad boy,* he concluded that, as a result, he could never have what he really wanted.

With repetition over the years, Lindsay wrote for himself a life script that was based on a lie. The script said he would never get what he wanted in life.

Perhaps you have written such a script, which you feel compelled to read and follow as you live out your life. You may be aware of it and readily tell others, to use Lindsay's example, "Oh, I wouldn't get that position. I never get what I really want. I don't deserve it!" Or you might be unaware of your script, with its controlling power unrecognized, until somebody mercifully helps free you from its control.

No one can understand why Lindsay would be lastingly wounded by this particular episode and certain others, or why Lindsay would have drawn this conclusion and added it to his life script. Someone else might not have been hurt or might have drawn a different conclusion. What we do know is that this happens, and the script needs to be rewritten (or the tapes erased and recorded with more truthful information) if healing is to occur.

Healing Your Wounded Personality

You will need help to rewrite a life script based on lies. It may be helpful to take some more 3 x 5 cards and write on them Bible truths that need to be in your script in the place of those lies. It was Psalm 37:4 that helped Lindsay: "Delight yourself in the Lord, and he will give you the desires of your heart."

It is important that you rewrite the script with the truth, especially scriptural truth, and not with wishful thinking. Many self-help books encourage this second option. Adherents of the New Age movement believe that we are gods with power to create our own reality. It is not surprising that they would encourage us to write anything we want in our scripts.

When we rewrite our script based on truth, it is important to remember two things:

First, you are not a god and in order to make a new reality happen, you have to rely on a power outside yourself. If that power is not God, then it is demonic. To reach out to spiritual power not submitted to God in order to acquire or achieve something is just a way of making a pact with the devil. The result is demonic bondage.

Second, you often do not know what is good for you, or what you really need. Little children want to eat candy, not vegetables. No amount of nutritional education will convince a sugar-hungry three-year-old to eat carrots instead. You and I are much the same. Much better simply to ask God for His help but leave the specific details to God. It may not have been good for Lindsay to be offered that particular position he wanted. This is something only God can know. But getting that position was not Lindsay's problem. His problem was thinking that he could never get *anything* good. Writing into the script words that affirm God's desire to give good things to him was the rewrite the script needed.

It is essential to recognize these twin dangers—demonic bond-

Free to Be Me!

age and settling for what you *think* you need instead of waiting for God to give you something better. Since many churches do not minister healing in intentional and effectual ways, hurting people are susceptible to New Age lies and their author, Satan, who masquerades as an angel of light (2 Corinthians 11:14).*

How do you know when you have adequately replaced the lies of the old script with the truth of God's script for you? By observing what happens when confronted with the kind of situation that triggered the old response. If your response—in thought or in action—has changed for the better, healing has occurred.

If you continue to work on this with God's help, the old lies may assert themselves, but they will no longer have power over you. Lindsay Warren told me that a year after a friend prayed with him for healing of the episode with his father, he had another disappointment. He said, "The old script came back: 'See? You can never have what you really want!' Now it was easy for me to say, 'I don't need that old script anymore.' "

Even better, and I pray this for Lindsay, is when his automatic response will be, "That's O.K. I know God has something different—and better—for me." It is important to note that for this to be a manifestation of divine healing, it must be a reflection of the new reality within, not an example of denial.

The seventh step in restoring your personality to wholeness is to renounce any misguided vows you have spoken or any help you have requested from spiritual powers not in submission to God.

Anyone who is hurting is likely to make wrong vows. Ruth was so ridiculed as a child for her intuitive daydreaming that she

---

* For further information on the contrasts between Christian and New Age beliefs and practices in the ministry of healing, see my book *Christian Healing*, chapter 8.

vowed never to entertain such nonsense again. She told God that such thoughts were childish. This prevented Ruth, however, from having that deep, personal, mystical relationship with God that rounds out Christian discipleship. (A balanced, complete walk with God includes belief in biblical doctrine, obedience to God's commands and a personal relationship with Him.) In addition, Ruth's vow had the effect of suppressing her God-given creativity.

Such vows have power, especially if made to God or any other spiritual being. It may be necessary to come before the Lord, perhaps with the assistance of a spiritually mature friend, to renounce these vows.

If in your pain you have called out to other spiritual beings, either to bring you comfort or to inflict pain on your abusers, you will have to renounce this and ask God's forgiveness, cleansing and infilling. Jim grew up a very practical young man in a home of creative literary types. While the home was loving, the others thought Jim to be a dullard for his lack of creativity. One day Jim decided to call spiritual powers down on his family. While Jim did not mean for anything serious to happen to them, nevertheless, until he renounced this naïve but real occult involvement, he was not able to experience much healing.

What I have described in this chapter are healing steps for those whose problems do not need long-term professional help. Some woundedness, however, is so deep as to require that kind of help. We should be highly suspicious of the advice that professional help is unnecessary if we just turn it all over to Jesus. This may sound good at first, because it exalts the loving power of Jesus and because we do know of cases where dramatic emotional healing does occur. But to demand that everyone, especially those whose woundedness is severe, be healed instantaneously is not only wrong, it is cruel. It has the effect of further victimizing those already harmed by the actions of others. It says, in effect, if you are not healed right now, you must not be cooperating with God. While that is true occasionally, there are many people of deep faith who just cannot get healed according to the timetables others set. Their experiences are like that of Job, who was abused at the hands of friends who thought they were helping.

Social anthropologist David Lewis, Ph.D., has published a very helpful book about the rate of healing at a John Wimber conference in Harrogate, England, entitled *Healing: Fiction, Fantasy, or Fact*. He differentiates between (1) total healing, (2) a great deal of healing, (3) a fair amount of healing, (4) a little healing and (5) no apparent healing. A little more than fifty percent of those who received prayer for inner healing of emotional wounds claimed that they received either total healing or a great deal of healing. This left some 49 percent who required more healing prayer. Apparently their healing will occur in a more gradual manner. See also Francis MacNutt, Ph.D., *The Prayer That Heals*, and his discussion about soaking prayer when healing is gradual.

If you have sincerely tried the steps outlined in this chapter and are still experiencing a deep woundedness, you are not letting God down if you go to a pastor or professional counselor for help, provided that the person you choose is centered in God and the Scriptures. In fact, God has given these individuals their gifts to help people with needs like yours. Seek them out. Continue to pray for and rely on the grace of God, make use of the ministry gifts He has given to other people and do the hard work that God expects of you. Don't give up! God needs you healed to reflect His glory to the universe and to be able to do your share of the work in extending His Kingdom on earth. And He wants you to enjoy a life that is more whole.

5

Communicating with Opposites

❖ In his dialogue "The Symposium," Plato tries to explain why people seek out persons with opposite traits. Originally, he says, man was whole and complete, but then got split in two. Ever since that split, our lives are spent searching for the other half of ourselves.

While we do not take this literally, it does remind us that people do tend to be attracted to others with opposite personalities. It is not difficult to understand why. Most people know their weak sides and wish at times things were different. This makes other people whose characteristics or qualities they lack more attractive. In addition, because the thoughts and behaviors of these others are different, there is an element of mystery and intrigue about them.

I once heard a woman talk about her boyfriend in this way: "My life is so ordered and predictable. That's O.K., but sometimes it gets *too* predictable. With Andrew, you never know what's going to happen next." Sometimes God puts people with those different from themselves so that they can all be broadened and, therefore, better equipped to serve people of all types in His name.

But, surprisingly, that which first draws different types together often becomes a major source of difficulty later. Andrew's girlfriend liked his unpredictable ways at first, but then the newness wore off. What was fun as an occasional treat got old as a steady diet. The next time I saw her she, while professing love for Andrew, was complaining about his zig-zagging through life.

You will be the richer if you can overcome the barriers erected by differences in personality type. Marriages and friendships can be strengthened as those stumblingblocks are removed. You can learn from others about that part of your personality that is not dominant.

That which hides in the shadows of your life can be seen more clearly when it is the dominant personality of another person. If it is true that as you get older this shadow side emerges, then to learn about it by observing it in others is important. Otherwise, when your shadow side emerges, you will be blindsided—that is, taken by surprise by the new and strange feelings, attitudes and actions. Better to learn about it as seen in a confident, mature version. Then, as in Plato's myth, you will be enriched by finding your other half, the part of your personality that is not dominant. You will be able to enjoy aspects of life you have missed.

As you learn how to make use of those less developed parts of who you are, you will be able to have a different angle on decisions. You will learn how to understand and relate better to all kinds of people, not just the ones most like yourself. You will find that working with others on a project is easier when you know how to make use of the strengths offered by the different personalities of fellow teammates or committee members. You will find ways of studying the Bible, praying and worshiping that suit you best. You will find much less frustration in a spiritual

Communicating with Opposites

style that is more authentically your own than someone else's.

In this chapter, we are going to examine various ways that an understanding of personality type will enhance interpersonal, one-on-one relationships. In the next chapter we will see how this applies to working with a group of people on a project or on a committee. Then we will see how this applies to our respective walks with God and how our churches can better provide a variety of spiritual growth opportunities.

Please remember, in each case I am talking only about the possibilities that are decent and godly. It would be incorrect, as some are doing, to make indiscriminate variety or inclusivity the goal. Some ways of thinking, believing and acting are wrong. They are unloving and fall outside of what is given to us by God in Scripture. As Jesus said, "The truth will set you free" (John 8:32). That which is not of the truth may sound interesting, and allowing it may *look* loving and inclusive, but it is ultimately harmful to ourselves and others and disobedient to God. It is nonsense to say, for example, that stealing is just a way that a perceiver demonstrates his or her easygoing nature or dislike of rules and structures. Personality type theory is not to be used as a way to rationalize wrong behavior or belief.

On the other hand, within the boundaries is a rich variety. The God who does not make two snowflakes alike did not all of a sudden start a cloning operation when it came to people. The New Testament shows that God calls a diverse group of people to serve Him, from the impetuous Peter, to the timid Timothy, to the scholarly Paul, to the mystic John. God gave a variety of personalities and our task is not to destroy that variety but to celebrate it. Growing into personal and spiritual maturity does not mean we become like other people. Rather, we become better and holier versions of ourselves for God's glory. If it is wrong to accept an overly generous inclusivity, it is also wrong to accept an overly restrictive narrowness.

Free to Be Me!

The key is biblical balance, as always, placing the same relative emphasis on complementary truths as the Bible does. Thus, we need to avoid the opposite dangers of being too broad and too narrow. There is a limit to the variety, yet within the boundaries God has set there is a lot of room for differences. By the way, a person's tendency toward being too broad or too narrow is often an indicator of personality type. While there are, of course, exceptions to this, those imaginative intuitives tend to err on the side of too much diversity or inclusivity and the detailed sensates on the side of too much narrowness or exclusivity. Feelers tend to err on the side of too much latitude, while the more dispassionate thinkers tend to be too narrow.

Remember, these are generalizations; exceptions abound. It is best to be aware of any way you tend to depart from the biblical balance. You need to watch and see if you are, in fact, departing from that balance.

I have mentioned already that when my wife and I dated, we found our almost totally opposite difference in personality types to be a serious, relationship-threatening matter. Mary is an introvert; I am an extravert. Mary is a sensate; I am an intuitive. Mary is on the borderline between thinker and feeler; I am a strong feeler. Mary is a strong judge; I am a judge in some things, especially in my teaching and writing, but a perceiver in many other things.

In terms of how we typically thought, acted and interacted, we were speaking two languages. No wonder we spent so much time discussing the discussion or asking, *ad nauseam,* "What did you mean when you said . . .?" Telephone conversations would often end with us both hurt or angry. We were just not communicating. We knew we loved each other and that God had brought us together, but could we stand a life together like this?

Thankfully, we were able to work through the problems and

Communicating with Opposites

build bridges over the barriers that our differences in personality had erected. We did this in a number of ways.

First and foremost, we offered ourselves regularly to the Lord, individually and as a couple, in surrender and in prayer for His divine assistance. That was of utmost importance, for without this, the other steps we took would likely have produced changes that were of short duration.

Second, we studied the matter of personality type differences. I had been working with the Myers-Briggs Type Indicator professionally for a few years and I asked Mary to take it to find out her personality type. It confirmed what we had already concluded, that we were almost exactly opposite in personality.

We used the various questions of the Myers-Briggs questionnaire as jumping-off points for discussion. A person who takes the MBTI, for example, is asked which he or she prefers when at a party: to sit in a corner with one person in deep conversation, or to circulate around having quick conversations with many people. Predictably, Mary and I answered this differently. We spent a while discussing why we responded the way we did, wondering aloud frequently, "How on earth could you have answered this question that way?"

These statements were not meant as put-downs. Rather, each of us was so used to thinking, feeling or acting in a certain way that it was inconceivable a normal person could respond differently! It was a helpful discussion, for while neither one of us was out to convert the other to the "right" way of doing things, we now knew more about how the other ticked.

Third, we looked at areas where our personalities had been wounded by the actions or attitudes of others, especially during our formative years. Then we asked God to heal those wounds.

Fourth, we looked for ways to deal with the inevitable differences that came up. Our desire was to find a third alternative.

Free to Be Me!

Sometimes, for example, I would drive from Boston up to Biddeford, Maine, where Mary was in medical school. I would let myself into the beach cottage in which she and fellow student Eileen lived. If I got there early I would sit by myself for some time reading. As an extravert, I can't go too long without the company of other people. As a feeler, I was especially looking forward to warm, friendly fellowship.

Sometimes Mary would come in the door and go almost immediately to her bedroom and stay there for a half hour. The extravert in me was left unsatisfied—I needed people contact. I had been by myself too long! The feeler aspect of me was crushed—what did I do wrong? Mary, the introvert, was "peopled out" all day at school and needed time to bring her energy level back up by being alone. I had my needs, but so did she. The problem was how to meet both of our needs.

We found the solution. Sometimes Mary would telephone me from school and say, "I love you and I miss you [that was important to me as a feeler] but I am all stressed out by today's activities. I'm going for a walk now to refill my drained batteries, but I'll be home in a half hour." On other occasions Mary might come in the door, kiss me and say, "I love you. It isn't you; I am drained. I'll be out in a half hour." Those statements kept my feeler side from feeling rejected—it wasn't I; it was the day's activities—and they said to me that if I really needed to be energized by people right at that moment, I could always go to a public place and talk with whoever happened to be there!

When sinful attitudes or actions are at the root of the problem, they need to be recognized, confessed and forsaken. But when the problem is solely a personality problem—as it often is—the search for a third way of relating that respects the rights and feelings of both persons is well worth the trouble. Perhaps you know of a couple like you and your spouse, at least in some aspects of personality. It might be a good idea to ask them how they build bridges over the chasms of personality type difference in their relationship.

Fifth, we learned how to speak each other's language. Often interpersonal problems have to do with communication styles. Different personalities have different ways of speaking and hearing.

By learning these differences, communication can be enhanced and relationships can be strengthened. Let's look in more detail at the art of communication between opposite personality types.

Extravert-Introvert Communication

While it is true that extraverts and introverts sometimes envy each other for possessing characteristics they wish they had, there is also hostility between the two personality types. I did not realize how much anger was there until I started conducting my personality type and personal growth seminars. I sent the extraverts off into one room and the introverts off into another and asked both groups to come up with a joint list of questions they had for the opposite group.

After the usual initial questions of curiosity, out came a growing torrent of anger. It seemed the two groups were just waiting for the opportunity to tell each other how frustrated and angry they were! The extraverts seemed to think that the reason for the introverts' silence and low energy was passive anger, that by saying nothing they were deliberately holding back. The introverts, meanwhile, felt the extraverts were trying to be in control by overwhelming them with words and energy. After the anger was ventilated, both groups welcomed assistance in building bridges across the personality type chasm.

Here are a few pointers in building extravert/introvert relationships.

Free to Be Me!

Extraverts

Extraverts can be described as cheerleaders of the game of life. They are usually loquacious, although there are quiet extraverts. They usually want to be where other people are, giving of themselves enthusiastically and participating heartily in what's going on. They want to get everyone to participate in whatever is happening.

We see the extravert in a child coming home from school, gleefully talking a mile a minute about the activities of the day. We see the extravert in a man running from his easy chair to the car because the radio said something exciting was happening downtown. We see the extravert in a woman going up to an individual standing by herself at the coffee hour after church because she didn't want her to be alone.

Many envy extraverts for that enthusiasm and the ease with which they engage others. One introvert told me, "I wish I could walk up to a group of people and start talking with them as Frank can." Another introvert shared, "I know I miss a lot but I find it very difficult to jump into things. I usually just ponder them from the sidelines."

Therefore, introverts, try to show energy and enthusiasm when you talk with your extravert friends, especially if what you are sharing is important to you.

I remember an incident with an introvert friend that brought this point home to me. He had been offered the opportunity to attend a prestigious gathering of people in his profession. For a man of his young age it was an honor to be asked. He shared this with me in a typical introvert fashion—low-key, quiet and brief. Then because of some personal matters that came up at the last minute, he was unable to go to the conference. When he told me that, I gave some offhand comment, intimating that I didn't think missing the conference was that big of a deal.

Communicating with Opposites

He was crushed! He accused me of being insensitive. He wondered how I, his friend, could so easily dismiss such a big event in his life; I told him I didn't realize it was a big deal. He told me that he had shared the invitation with me when he received it; I told him that had I received such an invitation I would have shouted it from the housetops, waved my arms wildly and talked nonstop to anyone who would listen. He reminded me that he *never* acted like that; and I told him that that was probably why, though hearing his words, I didn't grasp the meaning. After all, I said, had he won the lottery he wouldn't have said, "Oh, by the way [yawn], I just won three million." And he told me that he just might have!

He learned that in talking with me and with other extraverts, he needed to jump up and down a few times and actually raise his voice if he wanted us to catch the importance of what he was going to say. Otherwise we might hear his words but we wouldn't *really* hear him.

When talking with extraverts, try to use plenty of words.

As extraverts think out loud, they think it is normal to say things prior to coming to a definite conclusion or decision. They have no difficulty sharing their verbal scrap paper. When they talk with other extraverts they often just *semi*-listen during the first part of the conversation. They wonder why they should bother listening since nothing definitive is likely to be said. They tune in instinctively, however, when they sense the other extravert is starting to say things worth listening to.

Introverts, who process their thoughts internally, seldom speak unless what they are going to say has been well thought through. Therefore, if the introvert doesn't say much—nothing except the actual conclusion of the thought process—the extravert will probably not have tuned in yet.

Introverts need to make sure they have gotten the extravert's attention. One introvert friend of mine used to grab me by the shoulders, look intently into my eyes and say, "Mark, I'm going to say something now!" My lighthearted response was usually, "Behold, she speaketh!" Introverts need to let the extraverts in on the process of coming to a decision or conclusion. Sometimes I ask my introvert friends to "share your scrap paper."

When talking with extraverts, try not to allow long pauses. While reserving your right to ponder matters internally, at least let the extraverts know you are still in the conversation.

Sitting in the back seat of a car can be a wonderful opportunity to engage in personality type watching of those in the front seat! I recall riding for a few hours with a married couple. He, the extravert, would comment on the scenery. His introvert wife would say nothing. Finally, after several comments that had been left unresponded to, he turned to her and said, "Honey, are you paying attention?"

"Yes, I'm paying attention," she said. "Why do you ask?"

"Because you're not responding."

Her response to that comment was true to type for an introvert: "I didn't think 'Isn't that a pretty cow?' needed a response. What do you want me to say: 'Yes, dear, that is a pretty cow'?"

"Of course!" he said. "It doesn't have to be profound. It could even be just a grunt, but something to let me know you're with me in the conversation."

Time studies have been done on how long it takes extraverts and introverts to respond to a question. The average response time for an extravert is under two seconds! Mind you, they may not say anything profound at first. But they do start talking.

Introverts wait an average of over seven seconds—an eternity to an extravert—before saying anything. Many extraverts assume that if introverts are not saying anything, they are either bored, confused, want more talking from the extravert (seldom the case!) or are playing passive-aggressive games. While extraverts need to learn patience, an introvert can help by responding immediately with something like, "Interesting question/thought/suggestion/idea. Let me ponder it for a while and get back to you." This allows the introvert the opportunity to think it through in the privacy of the mind, while telling the extravert that what he or she said is being taken seriously. (It also subtly tells the extravert to shut up!)

Let extraverts think out loud. It's the way they do it. Growing up in the Boston area, I had the opportunity to know people from a number of ethnic groups. At least one of these groups talks with an energetic use of the hands. One day when I was talking to a friend of mine of this ethnic group, I grabbed his hands and wouldn't let him move them. He said, "Hey, if I don't use my hands, how can I talk with you?" We both laughed. He couldn't! The same is true with extraverts. If they can't talk out loud, they can't think!

For a number of months I was acting director of music at what was then my home church, St. Paul's Church in Malden, Massachusetts. On the weekends that I was not out on the road ministering, I would play the organ and direct the choirs. On the weekends that I was away, music was provided by the church's contemporary praise music group, led by Bill Deans.

Bill and I needed to check in regularly with each other for planning and coordination. As two extraverts, we would often bounce ideas out verbally, not just to get the input and feedback from the other person but also to engage in the verbal processing extraverts find necessary to think something through.

One day this went to such extremes as to be laughable. Bill and I met in the hall and both began to talk loudly and enthusiastically about ideas we had. We both went on, nonstop. At the end of fifteen minutes we looked at each other and said simultaneously, "Thanks, you've been very helpful."

Free to Be Me!

The group that had gathered to watch this spectacle burst into laughter. The introverts among them shook their heads wondering how on earth we could have been helpful to each other when neither one of us was listening to what the other had said. But helpful we were. All we needed was the presence of another warm body so we could get the mouths going and, therefore, the thought process.

Introverts

Introverts are the quiet people of the earth. They love the world within their own minds and the quiet places of life. They often know well how to keep and enjoy their own company. While they find it difficult to form new relationships at first, their friendships tend to be deep and long-lasting. They tend to enjoy ideas or concepts more than activities.

According to Myers-Briggs research, they account for only one quarter of the population in the United States, which helps explain why they often feel misunderstood. Introverts have told me that they feel much more understood in England, with its generally introverted culture. In this country, introverts often feel pushed aside.

For this reason, while both the extraverts and introverts express anger during that segment in my seminar devoted to extravert/introvert communication, the level of anger is usually much higher in the introverts.

This is not because the introverts are angrier people. Rather, it is because the extraverts do not have trouble finding other extraverts to relate to. After all, they make up 75 percent of the population.

In addition, the culture of the United States is geared toward them. Extravert bosses, in evaluating employees for advancement, do not often assume that silent waters run deep. As one introvert said, describing her boss, "Fred assumes that silent waters mean a drought! If I'm not saying things, loudly and frequently, he assumes I have nothing to say; and if I have nothing to say, how can I be qualified for advancement?"

Introverts also resent people who monopolize conversations and time. They often feel extraverts are inconsiderate for making them listen to their whole thought process whether or not the introverts want to—and whether or not they know the introverts well!

How can extraverts respond to this often appropriate anger introverts have, and communicate with them in a way that respects who they are?

Remember not to overwhelm introverts with noise and energy.

The volume of words that an extravert employs overwhelms many introverts. If possible, extraverts, do more of your thinking internally. Or, if you really need to think out loud, find another extravert with whom to do it. Don't do your processing at the introvert's expense. In a similar way, watch both your energy level and volume. These can overwhelm, even if you are not saying much.

Introverts tend to give the same weight to everything a person says and it confuses them that extraverts assume everyone knows the difference between processing a thought and coming to a conclusion. An introvert friend, exasperated with my verbal diarrhea, once said, "Mark, I don't know whether you are thinking out loud, sharing your conclusions or just running the verbal garbage disposal system!" Sometimes it is helpful to say to an introvert, "Let me think out loud for a minute." Or, if you have come to a conclusion, let the introvert know there is a difference between what you have just said and what you are about to say. Something like this might be helpful: "I've been thinking out

Free to Be Me!

loud on this for a while, but I believe I've come to a conclusion.'' If you don't do this, your introvert friend may be left bewildered.

Try to let the introverts think before expecting them to speak.

Being an extravert, I just assumed that whenever I asked a question, the other person would respond immediately. When somebody did not respond in a split-second way, I assumed that he or she had nothing to say, did not understand the question or was playing games with me. So I would ask the question again or rephrase it or add information or, if I wasn't in a good mood, demand to know why I was not being answered! Often the poor introvert would be left bewildered or hurt. As introverts deploy their energy inward much more than outward, seldom did they ever get energetic enough in their negative responses to get me to realize that I was being a jerk and should act differently in the future!

Finally I learned when asking questions of introverts to let them think first before speaking. That was a novel concept to me and I devised a plan to make sure sufficient time was given for them to think.

When I was in junior high school, I learned how to calculate how far away a lightning strike was. When you see the lightning strike, you count one-thousand-one, one-thousand-two, etc., until you hear the thunder. Each one-thousand count represents a thousand feet of distance between you and the lightning. I figured I could apply this to talking with introverts. I started counting one-thousand-one, one-thousand-two, etc., when asking them a question. I allowed ten whole seconds of silence before starting to get nervous at the silence. It often worked. A few of my introvert friends noticed the difference and told me that they appreciated it.

Respectful of the distance between themselves and others, introverts won't often intrude into that distance by volunteering information. But they do like to be asked, provided you ask only one question at a time! Do not assume that introverts are uninterested in what you are doing or saying. They may be taking time to think internally, or they may be waiting for you to invite them to share.

If possible, let the introvert get to know you and trust you over a period of time.

Introverts make friends slowly. This is especially true in making friends with extraverts. Introverts have had many bad experiences with extraverts overwhelming them. They want to make sure that you won't do likewise.

One of my favorite stories illustrates this. In *The Little Prince,* Antoine de Saint-Exupéry describes how to tame a fox. An extravert, upon seeing a fox, would think, *Oh, boy, a fox! I want to be his friend,* and run right up to the fox. The fox, being wily yet cautious, would disappear quickly into his hole. How does he know what the intentions of this person are?

Saint-Exupéry says the way to tame a fox is to go to a place a good ways off from the fox and just sit there. This lets the fox size you up from a safe distance. The next day go back and move only a bit closer. Sit there quietly and let the fox study you some more. Continue the process, each day sitting a bit closer. Eventually the fox has studied you enough to know and trust you. You have tamed the fox.

Introverts need to be "tamed" in the same way. Give them time to come to know and trust you. As relationships with introverts tend to be of a different order than those with extraverts, what they lack in immediacy and activity will be more than compensated for in longevity and depth.

Extraverts and introverts can communicate without anger and

Free to Be Me!

frustration as they learn the different worlds each inhabits and the languages each uses.

Sensate/Intuitive Communication

There is also a communication gap between sensates and intuitives. Sensates are the matter-of-fact people of life. We have already mentioned Sergeant Joe Friday on the television program "Dragnet" directing somebody he was interviewing to give "just the facts, ma'am." In other words, the detective was not interested in speculation. That was the job of the police department. What Joe needed from the witness was concrete, specific, hard evidence.

This is the orientation of the sensate. He or she tends to be good at detail and the matters at hand. Sensates deal with the specific and the real. They are not usually very good at fantasizing, often seeing it as a waste of time when something more practical could be taking place. Speculation about theoretical possibilities counts only if there is data to back it up and if it makes sense.

Do you remember Mr. Spock's regular comment to Captain Kirk on "Star Trek" when Kirk was giving some intuitive speculation? "Not logical, Captain," he would say. Sensates are the majority in America, comprising approximately 75 percent of the population according to Myers-Briggs studies. As with extravert/introvert, there is no difference in percentages between men and women.

Sensates

There are several things intuitives need to bear in mind when talking with sensates.

Attempt to state the matter simply, directly and in an orderly framework.

Communicating with Opposites

Don't give a lot of information or information that is not directly related to the specific matter at hand. Stephen was having trouble with his (intuitive) boss at work. "The boss always tries to show me how what I'm doing connects to what he calls the grand scheme of things. What I want from him," Stephen complained, "is for him to spell out the job, a, b, c. He gives me some deep blue sky explanation, using all these broad terms, when all I want to know is how to get the job done."

Whenever possible, show how what you are talking about is realistic and workable.

I have already mentioned the tinker-toy exercise I went through during my Myers-Briggs training. The structure we intuitives designed was beautiful and aesthetically pleasing, but when the sensates blew on it, it fell over! It worked in theory but it didn't work in real life. If you are ever to convince a sensate of the worth of a project, you must start by convincing him or her that it will actually work.

Two members of a church committee were looking into making their buildings wheelchair-accessible. Jim, an intuitive, was musing about how wonderful it would be for handicapped people to enter the church lounge from the parking lot without having to be carried up some stairs. That idea so captivated him that he went on for several minutes as to how many others might be attracted to their church, what other activities they could have and the like.

His reverie was shattered by the comments of Susan, a sensate, who pointed out that, given the tight squeeze of building and alley, a wheelchair ramp to the lounge would have to be so steep that few people could push a wheelchair up it! "We'll have to either build the ramp on the opposite side of the building or install an elevator," she pointed out. "But there's no way an outside

Free to Be Me!

ramp directly into the lounge will work." If it isn't practical, a sensate won't get excited about it.

Try to give examples.

While intuitives can usually grasp an idea given in broad, conceptual terms, sensates like specific examples. When Jesus wanted to get the point across, He used both concepts and examples. Let me give the sensates an example of what I mean! Jesus had just finished telling a lawyer that discipleship includes loving one's neighbor as oneself. The lawyer asked who one's neighbor is. Jesus, rather than giving a broad generalization, responded with the example of the Good Samaritan (Luke 10:25-37).

If you are trying to convince people of the advisability of a plan, give examples of how the plan has worked in the past in other settings.

A company was thinking about changing the way its stationery was printed and gave the job of coming up with alternatives to Ed and Warren. Ed, an intuitive, started bubbling over (in a quiet, introvert way) with various possibilities, focusing especially on no longer using a professional printing company but instead purchasing for themselves a high-quality, high-speed duplicator. Ed knew he was good at coming up with ideas, but also knew that for them to be accepted, especially by the sensates, ideas weren't enough.

After first sharing the concept with Warren, a sensate, Ed then proceeded to place in front of him examples of stationery from other companies that had made the switchover from professional to in-house printing. In addition, he presented figures of the cost of both ways of printing, demonstrating that the new way was cost-effective. He backed that assertion up with letters from the other companies documenting their savings. Warren was convinced and suggested they make a joint presentation to management. The intuitives came on board once they heard the idea, and the sensates thought it was a good idea once examples were presented and the assertion of savings was proven.

Attempt to show how any proposed change is an evolution from old ways, not a major change.

Although there are certainly exceptions, sensates give greater honor to traditional ways than do intuitives. There are a few reasons for this. Sensates are not as likely as intuitives to spend time speculating about what might be. They focus more on what already is. In addition, they have seen the folly of throwing out something that has been time-tested for something that is mere theory. But if you can show a sensate how your idea for change builds on what is already working well, keeping as much as possible of what has proven its worth, you will get a better hearing for those things you wish to change.

Intuitives

Intuitives are the brainstormers in our midst. They are the ones who like to think about possibilities, about what might be. They are the ones who shine in a brainstorming session where their creative, speculative, future-oriented bent can be given great expression. This is because intuitives are conceptually, rather than detail-oriented.

While sensates notice, often in detail, individual trees, intuitives are the ones who notice the whole forest, while sometimes missing individual trees. It's not that they are necessarily impractical. Rather, they are practical in other ways. Even though only a few of their ideas actually prove workable, still, were it not for these dreamers, we might not be enjoying nearly as many innovative ideas and inventions from which society benefits.

Free to Be Me!

Whenever possible, in speaking with intuitives, celebrate their creative imagination.

It is always an adventure to go shopping with Michael, my youngest child. His imagination is so vivid we often wonder if he just landed from another planet! Sometimes this can get a bit wearisome when I am asked, for the eleventh time, if I agree with some outlandish idea, like whether or not dogs would like to have pierced ears.

But leave it to Michael whenever we are stuck for an idea for a present for someone. Running thousands of wild ideas through his head, or trying to see how various combinations of things might work together (like cottage cheese and subway trains), sooner or later Michael comes up with an idea nothing short of brilliant. "I bet Nana would like that for her living room," Michael will chime in. "It is her color, it goes with the wallpaper, she has a knickknack of that shape in the room, she likes such-and-such a television program and they sometimes talk about things like this. . . ." And sure enough, Michael is absolutely right.

Sometimes people will joke and say, "With Michael you have to wade hip-deep through the nonsense, and then, just as you are ready to tune out forever, he comes out with the most incredible thought." With the Michaels of this world, while letting them know that it would not be a good idea to implement *every* suggestion they come up with, we need to praise their creativity and vivid imagination.

Try to show how the specific relates to the general; how the detail relates to the big picture; how the task affects the function.

Often my wife will ask me to do a specific task and I will surprise her by saying that I need more information before I can function, even at the most simple level. For me, it is important to know what the purpose of the task is, because I might do it in a slightly different way, or, if carrying out the task as assigned is not possible, I want to know the purpose so I can create a realistic alternative plan.

One evening Mary asked me to cut up some carrots and I said I needed more information. She looked at me as if I had suddenly taken leave of my senses. "What do you need to know more information for?" she asked. "Don't you know how to cut up carrots?"

"Yes, of course I do!" I asserted. "But I cut them one way for boiling in water, another way for steaming, another way if they are going to be finger food, and another way if they are to go with dip. In boiling or steaming, there are variations dependent on whether they are to be eaten *al dente* or cooked thoroughly. Then, it also depends on who they are for, because different people. . . ." On and on I went as only an intuitive who is also an extrovert can! Mary is learning that with me even such a simple task as preparing carrots has to be tied into the big picture.

Yet, don't direct the way the job should be done when talking to an intuitive. It would have been confusing had Mary told me specifically how to cut up the carrots. I would have been turned off by such specific detail and would much rather have figured it out for myself. When she told me how the task connected to the bigger picture—that she was going to steam the carrots for our dinner—I was all set.

Speculate as much as you can as to possibilities (a favorite intuitive word) in the future (another great word for the intuitive).

This may seem like a waste of time to someone who does not do a lot of speculation or thinking about the future, but it has the effect of engaging the intuitive in the task at hand. It is especially

Free to Be Me!

helpful if the intuitive has to do the kind of detailed routine work he or she does not usually like.

During high school and college I worked filling mail orders for a plastics company in my home city of Leominster, Massachusetts, the birthplace of the plastics industry. After a few days, putting the contents of one order—six boxes of #1066 comb, three boxes of #4628 barrette and four boxes of #9100 toothbrush holder—into a carton, sealing it and tossing it onto the conveyor belt, then filling a different order, then another, and another, got very boring. What saved it for me were Willie and Francis, the men with whom I worked.

Willie filled orders for smaller companies, Francis for large department store chains. Willie told me he often noticed the place from which the order came and speculated as to why people of a certain culture (say, small Southern town or wealthy East Coast suburb) would order certain products but not others, and why other locations placed different kinds of orders. Francis told me to imagine the McCrory distribution system with thousands of products coming to their central distribution points and going out to thousands of stores across the country. What would have been an otherwise boring job became filled with a number of possibilities for wild speculation, something this intuitive needed.

Like extraverts and introverts, sensates and intuitives can learn to understand each other and make themselves understood. And they can come to appreciate the different contributions each has to make.

Thinker/Feeler Communication

Extensive Myers-Briggs research indicates that in the United States thinkers and feelers each constitute roughly half of the population. Some sixty percent of men are thinkers; some sixty percent of women are feelers. There are those who believe that differentiation, the only sex differentiation in personality noted in the Myers-Briggs literature, is innate. That is, men and women are innately different emotionally. Others believe that this differentiation is due to cultural conditioning. That is, society expects men to be cool and logical and women warm and emotional. Until hard data is in hand, we have little more than speculation on which to base a conclusion. We can, however, be aware that, whatever the *cause* of the difference, society has conditioned us to expect men and women to be something that forty percent of them are not. This blindness is often a cause of woundedness.

Thinkers

Thinkers are the cool-hand Lukes and Lauras. They are not easily swayed by emotion or particularities of situations. They decide based on objective criteria, and want things to be just and fair. Seldom do they personalize a problem, either in themselves or someone else. A conflict is seen as a conflict of ideas, policies or goals rather than as a personal clash, anger or hurt. As a result they sometimes miss the people issues with which decisions are often intertwined. Here are some communication tips for you feelers.

In communicating with a thinker, try to be calm and objective.

Todd, a feeler, wanted to convince his wife, Margaret, a thinker, that serving wine at their upcoming dinner party would be a bad idea because one of the family members struggled with alcoholism. So concerned was Todd that in making the suggestion he got very excited. Margaret, true to a thinker's style, did not get caught up in her husband's emotions. Noting this, Todd wondered aloud if his wife cared. This got him all the more

Free to Be Me!

agitated as he started feeling more deeply what hurts could arise if his cousin starting drinking again.

"Don't you care about Lois?" he shouted at his wife. Margaret did care, and from the first sentence out of her husband's mouth she had started rethinking what they should serve. She wondered why her husband was so animated, and so angry.

Part of the problem in this conversation was that Todd, the feeler, had invested too much of his emotions into his suggestion. He was concerned for his cousin and he was well-attuned to the feelings of his family about her alcoholism. In talking with Margaret, he wrapped his laudable suggestion up with these emotions.

There is a lesson here for you feelers when talking with your thinker friends. Often thinkers, when presented with an idea or plan, will tell you exactly what they think. After all, you did ask for an opinion. Thinkers usually manage to keep emotional detachment from the thoughts or plans and cannot understand why pointing out the flaw in a plan upsets you so. After all, they criticized the *plan,* not you!

If you wrap yourself up in what you share, thinkers will not know how to respond. They will not be presented with something objective to evaluate, as much as a truncated series of half-facts and ill-articulated emotions. They will not know how to understand your feelings as it is not their dominant personality. Faced with this crisis, they will fall back on what they do best, be logical and objective. When that happens, you feelers perceive thinkers to be ignoring you or, worse, mocking you. All this does is engender *more* emotions from the feelers, confusing the thinkers even more.

While thinkers are not unfeeling, they often appreciate being shown love in practical ways.

Saundra, a feeler, was dating Brian, a thinker. Brian, working

120

Communicating with Opposites

overtime, had asked Saundra if she could pick up his VCR from the repair shop. Saundra picked up the VCR and went over to Brian's house the next afternoon to deliver it. She let herself in with the key he had given her and proceeded to fix Brian what she knew was his favorite dinner. When Brian came in she gave him a big hug and a kiss and told him how much she loved him. Brian's response was to look around and wonder aloud where his VCR was, crushing Saundra in the process.

For Brian, love is more an expression of practical, self-sacrificial service to another person than it is gushy emotionalism. No, Brian does not dislike emotions. He is not an emotional cripple nor does he have an emotional disorder. Rather, like most thinkers, he likes to express and receive love in more practical ways.

In talking with thinkers, you feelers will do well to talk to them about the feelings of others as a fact to weigh in their thinking.

We all have seen the skit with an American in a foreign country trying to get someone to understand him. When it is apparent the individual does not speak English, the American says the same thing all over again, only slower and louder.

Similarly feelers will try to get thinkers to be sensitive to their or someone else's feelings; when that doesn't seem to work, they just become more emotional. It is just as ineffective as the actions of that American abroad.

It is far better to attempt to explain feelings in rational terms. That involves translation, of course, not an easy thing to do. But it is important to try if you want to be heard.

As I write this, my wife and I just had an argument over the reactions of some firefighters whose firehouse was smeared with blood from an HIV-positive person seeking vengeance. Mary quoted several medical studies indicating how unnecessary it was

Free to Be Me!

to rip out and burn all the firehouse carpeting. My response was that, logic aside, those men were scared and that that fear was real and deserved attention. Mary was talking, coolly and logically, about the facts of the matter and I was trying to express how the men had *felt*. As she did not give any response to my statement about their feelings, I expressed my thoughts and feelings more loudly.

I would have done better had I said something like, "We must remember that the decision to rip up the carpeting in the firehouse may not be logical in terms of epidemiology, but it is logical in terms of the fear the men experienced. The decision makes sense from that perspective."

Feelers

Feelers often wear their emotions on their sleeves, and sometimes try to put them on other people's sleeves, too! They put great value on harmony between people and will often place that ahead of mere ideas. They feel both love and hurt deeply. They are the collectors of wounded animals and people and are very concerned about the happiness of others. Sometimes they set aside goals if they perceive that people might be hurt along the way.

In communicating with a feeler, it is important to establish the relationship before getting down to business.

Charles was a very good physician. He wasn't the best scientist *per se,* graduating in the lower third of his class at medical school. He never published a scholarly article and seldom made a presentation to his colleagues. They wondered, therefore, how he was able to come up with accurate diagnoses on complicated medical problems when they, the "better" scientists, often could not. They also wondered why his patients seemed to get better faster than theirs.

What these physicians, many of them naturally thinkers but all of them trained to *act* like thinkers, had forgotten was that part of the healing process involves caring. Charles always took a few minutes chitchatting with his patients, inquiring as to their family members, talking about the local sports teams, sharing his children's activities, before getting down to business. In being his patients' friend as well as physician, Charles earned their trust and they told him things they would not tell the more technically oriented doctors. This gave Charles clues as to the patients' diseases, and gave them the wellness-inducing sense that their doctor cared for them as people, not just as cases. While all patients, thinker patients especially, want to know their doctor is capable, feelers appreciate the personal touch.

Attempt to be more animated and emotional in talking with feelers.

To make a statement in a cool, calm way is not always enough if you want a feeler to hear you. Tanya, a feeler, received a letter informing her she had placed second in a national competition. She shared it with her thinker friend Rebecca whose response was given in gentle, measured tones: "That's good. Second out of all those people in the competition is quite an accomplishment." Although Rebecca expressed genuine appreciation in her comments, and as an extravert had no difficulty in talking, Tanya wondered if she really cared.

What would have communicated better? Had Rebecca been more emotional and given evidence that the thrill of this had grabbed the heartstrings, Tanya would have felt that her friend was really happy for her.

Remember, though, that communication with deep emotion has to take into account that not all emotions should be shared

Free to Be Me!

with the same level of intensity. Decades ago, Dale Carnegie wrote in *How to Win Friends and Influence People* that a secret to relationships is to be gentle with criticism and lavish with praise. Since feelers, like intuitives, often have high emotional investment in their ideas and plans, it is important, especially for thinkers, to give negative feedback gingerly. Before getting to the negatives, spend time on the positives. A word of caution: You had better be genuine in your praise, for a feeler's strong suit is emotion and he or she may detect phoniness.

There is sometimes mistrust between thinkers and feelers. Thinkers sometimes accuse feelers of being bleeding hearts, while feelers wonder if thinkers have hearts at all. I witnessed an argument between two people over the issue of replacing a dishwasher. Patricia, a thinker, wanted the old machine to go. "It is old, it sometimes leaks, it wastes energy," she told John, her feeler husband. "Let's get rid of it and get a new one."

"But it's the one my grandmother gave me," John replied. "It's not *that* bad. It only leaks occasionally and I'm usually right there to mop up. And what would the savings in electricity be a month? Ten cents? I'll pay it! It's just that the last thing I did with Grandmother before she died was to go shopping for this dishwasher, which was her Christmas present to me. It reminds me of her."

Who can say who is right in that situation? As a feeler, I can picture myself as John. My thinker friends cannot: "He's a sentimental mush. Can't he think of his grandmother in some way other than holding onto an inefficient old machine?"

Note that I deliberately selected a story in which the male was the feeler and the female the thinker. This particular distribution of personality types occurs frequently, despite the stereotypes. The issue of male/female roles can complicate discussion of a situation or else block discussion of the matter altogether. In this case, for instance, if I had described the woman as the feeler and the man as the thinker, society might dictate that the "logical, level-headed, thinking man" was making the wiser decision in getting rid of the machine, a reaction based not on the personality types of the individuals but on society's views of men and women.

I have conducted numerous counseling sessions in which a problem is kept hidden because one or both of the parties concerned would not share their thoughts and feelings for fear of being laughed at as being unmasculine or unfeminine. In fact, not a few of the people with whom I shared this story admitted they could understand the situation better had Patricia been the sentimental one who wanted to keep the machine and John the one who wanted to replace it. I pointed out to certain of my friends that they, of all people, should know how that sounds for they pride themselves on being modern and above the old-fashioned stereotypes of male and female. They were amazed at how deeply these cultural attitudes run.

In any event, the issue was not really the dishwasher. It was something deeper. So often the disagreement is not about the surface issue but about matters of how we view reality, perceive the world, value different things and so on. A friend of mine who has been studying personality type concluded, "I used to think the problem my wife and I were having was simply disagreeing about a decision. I now know the problem is that we disagree about how to decide!" This is why so many arguments do not get resolved. One person is arguing about the matter itself while another person, often unknowingly, is really arguing about some other issue.

For feelers, conversation is far more than sharing information. It is the sharing of hearts. This is why some feelers will tell the same stories or jokes over and over. They know that people have

Free to Be Me!

heard them already. In sharing these old stories, they are sharing themselves, and celebrating the depth of relationship they have with those whom they love.

This point is well illustrated by the old story (one I've shared many times with those whom I love!) about Abner, a Vermont farmer, and his wife, Flossie. The couple went in for marriage counseling. "Abner," Flossie started, "you never tell me you love me."

Abner said, "Remember what I told you on our weddin' night? I told you that I loved you and if this ever changed, you'd be the first to know."

Abner, a thinker (and probably an introvert as well), thought he had conveyed the information his wife needed to hear. Why repeat it? Flossie, the feeler (and probably extravert), knew the intellectual content of the communication that her husband loved her. She probably sensed by his devotion and fidelity he still loved her. But her *heart* wanted to be told again and again.

Thinkers and feelers have a problem in communication that needs to be overcome. When it is overcome, they discover that they bring different perspectives to situations. Thinkers keep feelers from moving so far away from objective fairness that they drown in a sea of subjectivity, or from being the victims of clever people with sob stories. Feelers keep thinkers from losing people on the way to achieving goals and from forgetting that emotions are important.

Judge/Perceiver

Judges are the structure-and-order people of life. They like to plan the work and work the plan. They see the value in orderliness and structure. People can count on the logic and order of whatever they do whether it is in their writings, their speaking or their organizing. They often accomplish a great amount because they will usually keep at the task until it is accomplished. Judges are ready to make decisions, accomplish tasks and move on to the next item. While judges find spontaneity, and sometimes even play, difficult, and while sometimes it is difficult to get them to break their routine, judges rightly deserve the nickname Old Faithful.

Therefore, perceivers, when talking with a judge, be ready to make a decision.

Judges will entertain new information but once they are convinced sufficient information is at hand, they are ready to decide and act. Don't dither or defer or a judge will sometimes pass you by or else dismiss you as a wishy-washy fence-straddler.

Martin was driving down a highway with his wife, Alice, one warm summer afternoon. They saw a sign for a tourist attraction several miles down the road and wondered aloud if they should stop. Martin was an introvert as was his wife, so he knew there would be a few minutes of silent pondering within both of them before anything was said.

After a few minutes, Alice started to speak. "You know, we could stop there, but then again, I wish we knew more about it. Then again, we might want to spend some time at another place. On the other hand, we could spend time at several places because it doesn't really matter whether we cross the state line tonight or not." Alice was not indulging in an extravert's run-on-at-the-mouth. Rather, she was exhibiting a perceiver's difficulty in making a decision. Martin really didn't care one way or the other what the decision was, as long as there was a decision.

"We'll be there in about four minutes," he said. "Just tell me, do we stop or not. That's all I want to know."

Try to give a judge warning when there will be a departure from the schedule.

Free to Be Me!

Surprising a judge with something at the last minute often stresses him or her. While this may make judges seem inflexible to perceivers, judges will make changes. It is just that they like to fit them into their plans ahead of time, if possible. And they don't want to have to do it too often. They find security in knowing that the universe, or at least the corner of it that has the most impact on them, is an orderly place. Why anyone would go against this security is beyond their understanding.

Dick worked at a lumberyard. His boss instinctively understood differences in personality. One Thursday afternoon the boss told Dick and his two co-workers there would be a change in the way the lumber would be stacked and explained the simple modification of procedure. The change would not take place until Monday.

A friend of the boss happened to be visiting when the boss spoke to Dick and his colleagues. "Why tell them now?" the friend asked. "That's a minor change, something they can adapt to in about five minutes. I would have told them Monday morning. Do they need almost four days to reprogram their minds?"

"No, they don't, two of them especially. Dick can reprogram immediately in terms of doing the work, but he likes it better if he has the weekend to think about and anticipate the change. I don't understand it, but I've worked with Dick for fifteen years. If it makes him happy to hear about it ahead of time, who cares? It's no big deal for me to tell him ahead but it seems to be important to him."

Judges appreciate knowing the plan.

On most things a judge does not mind what the rules or order happen to be. What is important is that there are a set of rules and a thought-through plan.

When I was in graduate school in England I would often visit the families of my fellow students during vacations. I didn't want to be rude as a guest in the homes of these people, gracious enough to house me for periods of time. I didn't mind what the specific customs and ways of doing things were in these homes. I was glad to adapt, but I needed to know. I never minded when someone pulled me aside and clued me in as to what was the right and the wrong thing.

In homes of perceivers there seldom were wrong things to do. Life was informal, even helter-skelter. Unless one was rude or horrid, it didn't really matter what one did. Although that was more difficult for me, I would eventually adapt. What was most unnerving was when there were customs and ways that should be followed, but I was not informed.

The best example of that was the time I stayed with an upper-class family. They had money, expensive possessions and hot and cold running servants. After the first meal was over, I proceeded to clear my place setting and head off for the kitchen—wherever that was!—to put the dishes into the sink. After all, that's how things were done in my middle-class Massachusetts home. I learned very quickly that that was *not* how one did things in proper British society! No one had told me. I finally cornered one of the staff of the house who explained to me, in very proper British butler tones, that I had invaded their territory. "There's the master and his family, sir, and the servants. If you do the things that appertain to the servants, you make our position tenuous. It is our job to wait on you, sir. If you wait on yourself, we are out of work and have nowhere to fit into the scheme of things."

I told him I understood (although I really didn't and still don't!) and would he be so kind as to tell me how I fit into that scheme of things since I had never been in a place like that before. He clued me in. He felt secure and so did I. Although there are aspects of that master-servant relationship of which I disapprove, at least I figured out how to behave for the rest of the weekend.

Free to Be Me!

Perceivers

Perceivers can be described as the playful ones, the puppy dogs of life. They are spontaneous, happy-go-lucky, adaptable. Making a decision can be difficult for them so they happily put it off. Accomplishing a goal might be a good thing to do; then again, why not defer for the fun of the moment? Perceivers seldom get hot and bothered about anything and so can be delightful people with whom to goof off. You judges need to allow for all of this in talking or working with perceivers.

Do your best to allow things to flow and develop on their own, according to the perceiver's timetable.

This can be extremely frustrating to someone who is goal- and clock-oriented, but it is hard to rush a perceiver. With a perceiver you must learn patience. Rather than yelling at a perceiver child who is invariably late, get him or her going way ahead of time. If you want a perceiver to arrive at a certain time, tell him to come a half hour or an hour earlier than when you really want him.

I have a friend named Tony. Recently when I was back in Boston taking a course toward my doctorate, I called Tony so we could get together. We were trying to find a time to meet. He suggested one o'clock one afternoon. I knew, given the time my class let out and the unpredictability of the Boston trolley and subway system, that I could not guarantee I would be in Cambridge right at one. Tony's response to that was, "No big deal, come sometime between one and two. You know me, I don't exactly follow schedules to the minute." Being a judge on these matters, I have a strong need to be punctual. Tony's statement was a relief to me—I could actually be a few minutes late.

Look for ways to allow spontaneity in the relationship.

David is, to say the least, spontaneous. Typically, he married

Ruth, a more ordered and structured person. David's idea of a vacation was to let things unfold. Ruth's was to schedule everything so that nothing would be missed. Neither appreciated each other's ways, especially during vacations. It got so bad they started taking separate vacations! Neither of them liked that arrangement and asked me for help.

Since Ruth needed structure and David needed to be spontaneous, I suggested this plan. On alternate days in the vacation Ruth should be in charge and David go along with the schedule, with no complaints. On the other days, David could be as spontaneous as he wanted to be. (And Ruth should write in her appointment book the word *spontaneous* in every fifteen-minute block!) It worked.

Try to let decisions be made in a different time framework, with last-minute changes expected and allowed.

While it may be frustrating to be with someone who is always changing his or her mind and deferring decisions, imagine, judges, what it must be like to be a perceiver around someone always making what seem to be snap decisions. Let perceivers have their different sense of timing as long as this does not translate into irresponsibility.

Judy is a strong perceiver and her boss, Miriam, is a strong judge. Miriam liked Judy and acknowledged that she did get results, "although I don't know how with a messy desk and a run-around way of doing things." Miriam would try to get Judy to conform to a schedule and Judy would always find it impossible.

Both attended a personality type workshop. During the final afternoon break they decided that there might be a better alternative to the standoff they had been experiencing. They were drained by it and nothing ever changed. Miriam communicated to Judy that as long as certain ultimate deadlines were met, the order

Free to Be Me!

in which the work was accomplished did not matter. Judy, for her part, agreed to communicate her progress so that Miriam would feel secure the deadlines would be met. Their plan worked well. Both the needs—and personalities—of Judy and Miriam were recognized.

Judges and perceivers can learn to get along, as Judy and Miriam did. And, like all the other paired opposites of personality, they need each other. We need the judges to arrange the flowers of life and perceivers to remind us to stop to smell them.

Recognizing and celebrating the diversity of personality can enrich our relationships. First of all, it means we can actually have a relationship with someone quite different in personality. The walls have been breached, the chasms have been bridged. Second, it means we have access to areas of life we might not otherwise explore were it not for our competent tour guide, someone of the opposite personality. Third, it means that those aspects of ourselves—those sides of our personality that are seldom manifest—can be embraced rather than feared. We can learn how to use them at the hands of those who know those sides well.

Mary and I still have times when our differences in personality get in the way, but by studying personality type theory we have the concepts to help us understand and appreciate each other. That and lots of love and prayer can work wonders in a relationship.

6

Working Better in a Group Setting

❖ Besides helping interpersonal relationships, an understanding of personality types can make a difference in a group setting.

All of us at one time or another are part of a group charged with completing tasks. It might be a task force at work, the executive board at church, a committee at our fraternal organization or a leadership team in some other context. If we are paying attention at all, we soon discover that issues of personality tend to crop up with a surprising degree of regularity. These differences can enrich the group by making it more representative of the larger group and by bringing to the task a greater spectrum of gifts, styles and perspectives. Or the differences can hamper or even thwart the group from reaching its goals. More than one group has gotten bogged down in the morass of interpersonal squabbles.

So the question is, how can an understanding of personality type enhance the work of the group and make it a pleasant experience as well? Or, put another way, how can there be mutual appreciation of the strengths coming from the differences in personality type, viewpoint and gifts?

Free to Be Me!

My first suggestion would be for the group to take a Myers-Briggs workshop and study issues of personality type.

While such a workshop is somewhat expensive and takes some time to do, it is well worth the investment. Church leaders have told me that the insights gained have made the working of the leadership much more harmonious, efficient and productive. (See page 223 for the names and addresses of Myers-Briggs–oriented organizations.)

A particular company was experiencing difficulties in the executive suite. Its twelve-person leadership team was composed of people who were all strongly committed to the success of the company, but who were also different from each other. Their internal squabbles were starting to affect the well-being of the company. It looked as though the problem might be resolved by firing some people. Fortunately, one of the members knew about personality type theory and suggested the team spend a few days working with a consultant.

The consultant first gave everyone in the leadership team the Myers-Briggs Type Indicator. The consultant then established the team type (Kummerow and McAllister, *Journal of Psychological Type*, volume 15, 1988, pp. 26-32). He discovered that the majority of the team fit the types of extravert, intuitive, thinker and judge, yielding a team type of ENTJ. This does not mean that the majority of individuals all had the specific personality type known as ENTJ, but that the majority fell into these four categories. This is important because a team will often develop a group personality type.

Then the leadership team studied the ramifications of personality type on their interpersonal relationships. They found that personality type language proved helpful in unearthing and explaining problems that had previously remained under the surface. One man, a sensate, now was able to understand that some of his feelings of unease with the group were not because of latent racism or sexism, but because other members of the group, especially the two black and three female members, were strong intuitives.

Second, I recommend adopting some ground rules specifically designed to help each person make a contribution and feel that being on the committee is worthwhile.

The suggestions that follow are gathered from the experiences of a number of church executive boards (consistory, vestry, cabinet, council, etc.) that have responded to my encouragement to develop procedures that would maximize each person's contribution. If you are in leadership or serve on a committee you might find many of these procedures useful. Should you come up with others, I would like to hear from you so others may benefit from what you have discovered.

Extraverts and Introverts

Because of the different ways extraverts and introverts process information and share that with others, some procedures are in order to make sure the extraverts do not dominate and the introverts do not feel like excess baggage.

In a parish I once served, I wondered why a certain person ran for the vestry (our chief lay governing board) because he never said even one word at any of the meetings. Other members wondered that, too. One even said to me, "We love Alan and we know he works hard for the church and is quite devout. But he's taking up a seat that should be filled by somebody who has something to say."

One day, a few days after a vestry meeting, I needed to call Alan on an unrelated matter and just happened to say, "What do you think about that proposal Melanie made?" Alan gave me about fifteen minutes of solid, lucid reasoning and ended with a recommendation that I thought was first-rate. My relationship with Alan was such that I could say to him, "Alan, what you just told me sounds like you've been pondering this for a while. Why didn't you share this the other night?"

His response? "Couldn't get a word in edgewise, and besides, nobody asked me." Later Alan told me he was thinking of resigning from the vestry, not because he wasn't interested, but because he couldn't figure out how to say what he wanted to say! From that point on I became determined to find ways to get everybody on board.

Starting with the next vestry meeting, I made it a policy to telephone within 48 hours all the vestry members, but especially those who were quiet at the meeting, and ask for their feedback or input. I was astounded at how much was said, and how grateful the introvert members were for being asked and given ample time to respond in their own way and time.

Another church tried this: After a discussion had been going on for quite a while, the chairwoman said, "For the next fifteen minutes the only people holding the floor will be those who have not yet shared." She left plenty of time for silence and immediately ruled out of order the talkative ones who were ready to jump back in. This brought out the quieter ones who either would not or could not get the floor by pushing into the conversation.

In the past, she would often ask at the end of a discussion, "Anybody else have anything to say?" When she did that either she would not allow enough time for a response before going on to the next item, or it would be an additional occasion for the dominant ones to speak further. She found her new way of doing things worked better.

The property committee of one church found something else that made their meetings go better: The chairman would mail

Working Better in a Group Setting

each member a letter containing the items that would be discussed at the next meeting with a lengthy discussion of the pros and cons as he saw them. Members were invited to compose their own letters, which were read aloud at the meeting.

I was invited in as a troubleshooter for one church vestry where the introverts and extraverts all got their chance to speak but the manner in which they did alienated each other.

The extraverts in this group were strong extraverts and were highly verbal and energetic when they shared. The introverts were strong introverts and felt that anyone that noisy or demonstrative must have a weak argument. ("You know the old joke about the marginal notes on a pastor's sermon?" one of the introverts asked me. "Argument weak. Shout like crazy.")

The extraverts, on the other hand, wondered why the introverts felt hurt that none of them took their arguments seriously. "Whenever they say anything," one extravert said, "they speak as quiet as a mouse and hardly ever even move in their chairs. How can I take seriously the views of somebody who appears to be bored with them himself?"

I worked with them to try to encourage both groups to meet in the middle. We practiced having the extraverts speak softly and gently and introverts speak loudly and animatedly. The high point of the evening was when an introvert who was also a jokester held up the sign written in tiny letters, "I *AM* SHOUTING!!"

Because introverts make up only 25 percent of the population, it is much less likely that an extravert would feel like the odd one out in a committee. But it does sometimes happen. I took a graduate school course recently and discovered, to my horror, that it was a class full of introverts! I was not able to think out loud in a group setting to the degree I like. I coped by finding the few other extraverts in the class and having think-out-loud sessions during the breaks and after class. The conclusions reached in those sessions were presented during class. I also found that my comments were taken more seriously if I presented them in a less verbose and animated way. It was good practice. It was also the occasion for me to share with others some personality type theory. I suggested that, as I was a minority in that setting, they should make allowances for the way I think and discuss. I didn't push that point too far because I realized it was probably one of the few times the introverts were running the show.

Sensates and Intuitives

Remember, sensates are the detailed people who look at things from a practical point of view. They look at specific details and ask the question "Will it work?" Intuitives are the idea people who see the big picture. They ask the question "What are the possibilities?"

I was once in a committee in which the sensates and intuitives did not appreciate each other in the slightest. The sensates always thought the intuitives were impractical dreamers. "They'll bankrupt us yet with all their crazy ideas. None of them will work!" one sensate said.

"But if we listened to those sensates," an intuitive replied, "we would never make any progress. If you aim at the ground you'll hit it every time. Of course some of our ideas are impractical, but what ideas do they come up with?" Obviously this group was not aware of the strengths, only the weaknesses, of the people of opposite personality type.

One leadership group, the executive committee of a Boy Scout troop, found a way around the dilemma of personality type clash. In addition to recognizing the strengths of sensate and intuitive personalities (although not calling them by their formal names), they agreed that the purpose of a meeting would be stated up front

Working Better in a Group Setting

so everyone would know what kind of contributions would be more appropriate.

"Let's make the next meeting an idea meeting," the Scoutmaster said. "We'll brainstorm for a while. No evaluation, criticism, discussion. Just ideas. Then we'll take these ideas and vote on the three we think can be best discussed and evaluated. We'll save that for another meeting."

When it was time for that idea meeting, as the Scoutmaster called it, he went over the ground rules for such a session. Perhaps you are aware that the first rule in a brainstorm session is don't evaluate, just articulate.

Once an idea has floated out, it is easy for people, *especially sensates*, to begin criticizing immediately the practicality or workability of the idea. Since the imagination is so precious to intuitives, criticism of an idea often hurts their feelings and dries up their creative juices. In addition, the focus of the meeting has changed from throwing out dozens of ideas to evaluating just one idea. Something wonderfully creative—and highly practical—may be kept from coming forth. Rather, let the ideas come forth, by the hundreds, perhaps.

At the end of that particular brainstorming session, the Scoutmaster affirmed the intuitives by saying, "We really came up with a lot of possibilities today! Don will send us a memo with each of the ideas described in a sentence or two. You let me know which three you would like to discuss further and I'll tabulate the votes. The top three will be discussed at the next meeting. If none of them yields anything we would like to implement, we'll look at the next three and so on. I bet one or two new directions will emerge from this that will really help the troop. Good job, folks!"

Had the Scoutmaster not known anything about the personality of intuitives, or had he been insensitive to them, or had he not known that even the best inventors test and discard many ideas on the way to finding their great inventions, he might have said, "Ninety-nine percent of the ideas tossed out today are nonsense!" Many intuitives know that their speculation-to-market rate is about one percent. There is no need to deflate their enthusiasm or wound them by punishing them for it. Instead, affirm their creativity.

When it was time to evaluate the top three ideas, the Scoutmaster showed further wisdom by reminding the group that those who suggest an idea often have great emotional investment in it. "So be gentle, folks," he said. "Don't say an idea is stupid, just say you don't see how it will work. And remember, just because *you* don't see how it would work doesn't mean it won't work."

Intuitives remind us that God is a God of miracles. God can do impossible things. I know of a small charismatic church that believed God wanted them to have a Christian radio station. Given the size of the congregation, the number of secular groups wanting to acquire the one available radio station license and the huge financial costs involved, it seemed like an impossibility. Yet they were firmly convinced God would do it, and He did. Instead of telling God the size of their problem, they told the problem the size of their God!

And yet not every great idea is from God, even if it makes us feel holy and would do a great thing for the Kingdom. It is beyond the scope of this book to list various ways of discerning God's will, but suffice it to say that the issue of being practical cuts right across the matter of discernment. Sometimes God tells us to ignore the practical difficulties and watch Him do something incredible. On other occasions, God uses the practical matters at hand to close a door we would like to go through. Jesus reminded His disciples how foolish were the men who started building a tower without first counting their bricks (Luke 14:28-30).

Both intuitives and sensates can be used of God; both groups can be mistaken. But when both are submitted to God, are trying to submit to God's wishes and not their own, and are sharing freely together, appreciating the gifts (and differences) of each other, the group's objective can often be achieved.

Thinkers and Feelers

Here is a speculative story about a thinker, the one who makes decisions on the basis of objective criteria, and a feeler, the one who makes decisions on the basis of personal issues.

One mid-sized city in the East had two companies that made hair combs. Both were locally owned family companies. Fred Cooke, of Cooke's Combs, and Richard Hare, of Hare for Your Hair, both in their mid-20s, were childhood friends as well as management trainees in their respective family businesses. One day they met at a pub to share what it was like now that they were part of their companies' executive committees. They both discovered they were uncomfortable.

Fred Cooke was one of just two feelers in a team of thinkers. "They're cold, task-oriented, competitive!" Fred complained. "They are crying out for emotional support but they don't give it to each other. They wonder why middle management and shop-floor workers are disgruntled and complaining that they don't feel appreciated. I'll tell you why. It's because they make their decisions based on good *business* sense but not on the basis of good *people* sense. I try to point out why, but I'm dismissed as young and naïve, although I do get through to them periodically. Good thing I'm family, or I would have gotten fired long ago!"

Fred's turmoil seemed to Richard to be a significant improvement over what he was experiencing at his family's company. "They're all so touchy-feely," Richard explained. "And Dad's the worst! He's always talking with the employees to see how

Free to Be Me!

they are. He's always bringing the management to a retreat center for a day where anything except business can be discussed. He's tending to everything but business! And when he finally gets down to business, he's so concerned that everybody expresses an opinion that decisions are not made efficiently. I try to get them to settle down to business before we lose our business, but they just smile at me and tell me to loosen up."

Fred and Richard wondered if perhaps they were born into the wrong families! They humorously suggested that they swap jobs. While that certainly would make Fred and Richard more comfortable and remove burrs from under two corporate saddles, they are exactly where they need to be.

Cooke's Combs needs to realize what many other businesses forget, that people problems are business problems, and that being good to people is good for business, not to mention the obligation God imposes on those having power and possessions.

At the same time, the Hare family needs to understand that sometimes if they refuse to make the tough decisions for fear of inconveniencing someone, or if they so attend to people that they fail to attend to the bottom line, one day their business may go bankrupt and then all those people they care about will be out of work.

Fred and Richard are where they need to be as minority voices crying out with views that should be seen as complementary, not contradictory. The question is, will the others catch on?

While any of the pairs of opposite personality types can cause difficulty when put together in a team setting, the thinker vs. feeler clash involves a deep core issue in Christian circles. Christianity deals with both truth and love. In any given Christian there is the tendency, sometimes mild, sometimes pronounced, to slip into favoring one side of the equation over the other. While it is not always the case, thinkers tend to stand for sound doctrine and feelers for compassionate love. As both of these are central issues in our religious life, commitment to one or the other can lead to problems with those emphasizing the opposite.

Thinkers

Jesus taught the necessity of the truth, which alone sets a person free (John 8:32). When coming into a group of Jews with differing views—for example, the Pharisee vs. Sadducee dispute over the resurrection—Jesus never spoke approvingly of the wide variety of beliefs in Judaism. He gave them the right answer!*

For the Church to be faithful to Christ, she must be concerned with the truth. While there is legitimate diversity of style in Christianity (something we will examine in the next chapter), there is not a legitimate diversity when it comes to sound doctrine. Both thinkers and feelers can guard this orthodoxy, but in doing so will usually come across differently.

Sometimes thinkers can seem cold and heartless even though they are not necessarily this way. (Similarly, feelers can seem warm and caring when they are not.) Thinkers can be very concerned for others' well-being, but they express it differently. Thinkers know that sound principles, dispassionate justice and applying the rules fairly will help everyone. Just because thinkers don't show emotion does not mean that they have no deep concern.

More confusing to feelers are those thinkers, a minority to be sure, whose contribution is diminished because of personal is-

---

* For a thorough investigation of this, see John R. W. Stott's book *Christ the Controversialist*. Stott's point is that Jesus always entered into the controversial issues of His day, theological and ethical. Far from commending a latitude of opinion, Jesus revealed the truth and expected His followers to change their thinking and behavior accordingly.

sues. As expressed by those people where fear, prejudice or personal insecurity is dominant, orthodoxy can become oppressive legalism or narrow fundamentalism. For many, especially feelers, this can give the quest for Truth a bad name. These cases are, however, aberrations and should not put us off to the important, Christlike role thinkers can hold. They keep us centered in the truth and remind us that any compassion at the expense of the truth ultimately does no one any good, and, therefore, is not loving.

Feelers

Feelers are the opposite side of the coin. In the Church feelers understand that of faith, hope and love, the greatest of these is love (1 Corinthians 13:13). They know, and want the Church to exhibit the fact, that God does not just *have* love, God *is* love (1 John 4:8, 16).

Feelers are concerned with people who are hurting and, in Jesus' name, want to reach out to them. They see Jesus approaching people whom the pious and proper Jews shunned. They witness Jesus refusing to condemn the woman caught in the act of adultery, and reaching out to the ostracized woman at the well. Feelers want the Church to reach out with similar love to the outcasts of today's society, who are no different from the marginalized people of Jesus' day. They know that since we, too, are sinners, we have no right to condemn. Feelers wonder how Christians can be unmoved at the sight of poverty and homelessness and not respond in loving, concerned ways.

The problem here is that feelers can be so concerned with expressing compassion to those who hurt, they allow or even reinforce the harmful or sinful behavior that led to the problem in the first place. They forget that often love must be tough love. In some cases, feelers see truth as an enemy that enslaves or categorizes people. Such feelers may make statements like, "People are more important than mere ideas or rules." But this is an aberration of love and should not put off others, especially thinkers, from the duty of the Church and of all Christians to love in Jesus' name.

Thinkers and feelers need each other desperately. Sadly, the polarization in the Church between pietists and activists, between conservatives and liberals, between those who emphasize sound doctrine and those who want to reach out to the oppressed, has tended to make both groups unbalanced. Reacting against the real or perceived errors in the opposite side, many become even more extreme.

I know some conservative Christians who are so angry at the permissive, anything-goes-as-long-as-we-are-inclusive pronouncements of some liberals that they have turned their backs on people with AIDS, unwed mothers and the poor. I have heard these people say, "They brought it on themselves." It is often true that one suffers because of one's own sinful actions, but this was also true in Jesus' day and He ministered to those individuals with love and compassion while calling them to the new birth and a new life.

Likewise, I know some liberal Christians who are so angry at the judgmental, self-righteous stance of some conservatives that they consider biblical truth oppressive! I have heard these people say, "The Bible was written by males, two thousand years ago, and has nothing to say to us today. It's a book of oppression. The Church is better off without it." Again, while it is true that some conservative Christians misconstrue certain passages of Scripture to their own advantage, that is no reason to cast aside the commands of Christ and the written Word that God has given as our authoritative guide.

Free to Be Me!

Sometimes reactions between these two groups are quite different. Instead of becoming angry at those who hold the opposite view and growing more extreme in their own views, some people turn off to their own group and flee in the opposite direction, often becoming just as extreme. Conservative Christians suddenly abandon their tightly held doctrine and announce that in the name of love anything goes. Liberal Christians conclude that their pursuit of love has ignored the moral teachings of Jesus and that sinners are out of luck if they expect any compassion.

Sometimes I feel as if I am standing on a street corner watching two groups of people fleeing for their lives. I want to shout, "Stop! You are leaving one extreme for the other. Balance is hard, but balance is what we are called to. Conservatives, you are right in demanding more compassion and less judgment, but do not abandon the truth. Liberals, yes, you have now discovered the truth, but don't abandon your compassion."

In Ephesians 4:15, we are exhorted to speak the truth in love. I admire those congregations who work hard for this. These Christians know that truth and love can be complementary—if done under the authority of Scripture and the grace of the Lord.

In that sense, there can be a biblical conservatism and a biblical liberalism, although we have too often seen only their secular versions in the Church. Biblical conservatism conserves biblical truth but is open to change on things that are not fixed by God. It holds to the Word, but is loving and compassionate to others. Biblical liberalism is open to applying the Word to every situation where compassion is called for. It shows that maintaining God's love and compassion, especially to those whom society is indifferent to, does not depart from what God has revealed.

This is a difference not of substance, but of *degree* or *emphasis*. Because we often see self-indulgence masquerading as freedom from biblical constraints, or uptight judgmentalism masquerading as biblical dogma, we forget that.

Let's look at two examples of how thinkers and feelers approach a balance of truth and love.

The elders of Hilltop Church had a dilemma. Theirs was a new congregation, formed from a number of families that had left the fundamentalist congregations in town. "Too judgmental," was the consensus of the founders. "We want biblical truth, but also biblical love."

The adults coming to Hilltop were recent, enthusiastic converts to Christianity, but their children were not. The parents very much wanted their children to come to the Lord but so far nothing seemed to be happening. The junior high children went to Sunday school and youth group not because they shared their parents' enthusiasm for the faith, but because they liked Josh, the youth minister.

Josh came to the elders with a question that weighed heavily on his heart: "What are we going to teach the children about sex? My problem is this: To the best of my knowledge none of them has given his or her heart to the Lord. They're here because their parents make them come and because I do lots of fun things with them. So should I present abstinence to them in the context of submission to God's will? Tell them that God gives us grace to maintain chastity? Frankly, obeying God isn't that urgent to them. So should I also approach it from the angle of disease and pregnancy? Assume they are going ahead anyway and inform them about preventive measures and safe sex?"

After some minutes of prayer, the elders started to ponder Josh's question. Al, a thinker, maintained that to say anything about safe sex would convey the message that this was O.K., no matter how much Josh said it was outside God's will. Several of the elders agreed with him. "The Word of God is clear on this subject," they said, "and our job is to raise the children in God's ways. The chief reason people were put on earth is to be disciples. Our children need to learn that God's ways are best, and lead to freedom. Anything to the contrary would undermine this message."

Cliff, a feeler, said that he understood all the pressures the kids were under. "We don't want to talk to them in such a way that, should one of them make a mistake, he or she will not tell us for fear of being disowned. Besides, their maintaining chastity ultimately has to be something they offer to the Lord as a decision of their own wills, not something imposed from without. That's the kind of legalism that drives people from God and, in fact, drove some of us to start Hillside Church. I think the kids should be told about safe sex, while hoping and praying they choose abstinence. But if they don't choose abstinence, we don't want them to get pregnant or, God forbid, AIDS."

I do not know how Hilltop Church resolved the matter but the discussion followed along the lines listed above. Discussions like this take place in churches all around the world, at least where the thinkers have not driven out all the feelers or vice versa.

Here is another example where the matter at hand was not so supercharged as the one of sex.

Glenn, a high school student, was taking classical organ lessons. He asked the trustees of his church for permission to practice on the church organ two afternoons a week.

The thinkers on the board of trustees examined the issue in classical thinker style: They looked at the issue irrespective of the young man. "There's the matter of liability in case something happens to either Glenn or the organ," Thurston, the chairman, began. "Then there's the precedent we are establishing. Others may want to do this, too."

The feelers on the board of trustees weren't interested in any of this. Their basic concern was Glenn himself. Grace said, "Glenn is a good boy. His parents have been members here for years. His feelings would be hurt if we said no. Shouldn't we try to meet the needs of our parishioners, especially our young people?"

Unfortunately the discussion did not proceed in Christian charity. Grace accused Thurston of being hardhearted. "All that matters to you are issues, not people," she said.

Thurston reminded Grace that charity in the past had led them into trouble. "Always a sucker for a sob story, aren't you, Grace? Remember how Larry rented the fellowship hall for his judo club? Larry's parents are members, too, but they have yet to pay for the damage Larry and his friends caused. And then there was that incident with Susan tutoring those high school dropouts. We have to be good stewards of the property or soon it will be all a shambles."

And so the discussion went. At the first signs of an impasse the committee might have turned to prayer, asking God for both His wisdom and His love. Instead, the argument escalated. They did not look for, much less find, a third alternative combining the best of Thurston's and Grace's insights. The answer to Glenn was no.

Thurston told Glenn and his parents the decision. Although they were mature enough to accept a negative answer, Thurston was not sensitive to their feelings in the factual way he relayed it. Glenn and his parents left that church and attended another, one that welcomed the young man to come use their organ and appreciated his ability to fill in for their organist on certain occasions.

Yes, thinkers and feelers need each other, but they must learn to recognize their respective strengths and weaknesses. Together, they can find ways to live out God's truth in God's love.

Free to Be Me!

Judges and Perceivers

The differences between judges and perceivers in a group setting, while not as significant as the differences between extraverts and introverts and thinkers and feelers, can, nevertheless, cause people to become annoyed with each other if the group is not careful. For some judges, it can be stressful to work with perceivers in a job environment that has regular deadlines—a newspaper office, for example.

Judges, remember, like order, structure and conclusion. They know that schedules guard against important things being left undone and last-minute confusion. They know that formulating and stating expectations clearly guards against feelings being hurt. Judges believe that bringing a matter to resolution is important. "We have gathered data and discussed it from several angles; now let's make a decision" is a judge's creed.

Perceivers, on the other hand, like to keep things loose and open. They know that sometimes God brings surprises, and that these surprises can be lost if everything is locked up far ahead. Perceivers know that stopping for a minute to regroup is no big deal, and certainly not the confusion that judges think it is. Perceivers wonder if too much scheduling and deciding can cause a person to miss the fun. "Let's leave it open and see what happens" is a perceiver's motto.

Because the trustees of Calvary Baptist Church oversaw a large congregation, they felt it wise to have set policies on a number of matters. "That way, everyone knows what is expected and there are no hurt feelings," they concluded.

Bob, their new pastor, had always served small congregations where everyone knew each other and where, as a result, decisions were made more informally. Pastor Bob thought this was more in

Working Better in a Group Setting

keeping with the way families decide things and, after all, isn't the church the family of God?

People liked Bob's informality, and the congregation responded well to his leadership for the first six months. Then problems arose.

One evening, for instance, two groups showed up to use the church parlor, both having been offered the space by Bob. That confusion was settled amicably as the smaller group agreed to use a different room. The next morning Richard, one of the trustees, expressed concern to the pastor. "Last night someone was in the parlor and in classroom three. I checked everything carefully. It didn't look like a break-in."

When Bob told Richard that he had told two groups they could use the spaces, the trustee became upset. "It wasn't on the schedule, for one thing," he said. "And did you give them the list of rules and expectations? They didn't turn down the heat, a light was left on, and heaven knows what kind of headaches we would have had if the doors hadn't been locked afterward. We've had a lot of problems here, Bob, and have established these rules accordingly."

Bob was hurt by this criticism. He had to agree with Richard, but something left him uneasy. He wasn't very good at following strict procedures, keeping schedules, holding people accountable to rules or planning way ahead. He wondered if he had made a mistake accepting the call to Calvary Baptist Church.

He shared that with his secretary. Irma was a spit and polish kind of person and he guessed she would agree with that thought. Much to his surprise she said, "Oh, no! You're exactly what this church needed! We'll have to work with you about procedures and policies or, better yet, get you to refer all requests for building use to me. But your informality has brought a breath of fresh air to this congregation. Everybody's talking about it."

Free to Be Me!

Irma explained further that the previous pastor had been a godly man who tended to be *all* procedures and policies. One Sunday morning when the person scheduled to make an announcement from the pulpit didn't show up, the pastor never said anything, but, according to Irma, you could cut the tension with a knife.

"When he came here," Irma concluded, "that pastor brought wonderful administrative gifts this congregation really needed, but once things got shipshape, we started noticing his weaknesses—he couldn't be spontaneous if his life depended on it!"

Pastor Bob wondered aloud about meeting with the trustees to discuss a leadership arrangement that used everyone's strengths. It was left to Irma to get him to schedule a date for the discussion!

That same month, across town, the executive board of the men's club had a decision to make. They had been using the guild hall of St. Ann's Episcopal Church for their meetings, but soon the hall was going to undergo renovations. The club would be displaced for several months.

"It's now March," Louis, the club's president, said. "We can have the hall until June. We don't meet in July, so August is not that far off. We have two proposals before us. The Methodist church has offered us space at fifty dollars a night. It's a good rate but the kitchen facilities are limited. Knox Presbyterian will charge us seventy-five dollars a night but the kitchen is first-rate. If we don't make a decision by tonight, we could lose one or more of those options. I propose we discuss and then decide."

Craig, a perceiver, didn't think this was a very good idea. "Look, St. Ann's was going to remodel a year ago and then put it off. Maybe they'll put it off again. We all know it's the best place for the best price. Then again, there may be other possibilities around town. August is a long way away. I doubt we'll lose the offers from these two churches, and even if we do, something

Working Better in a Group Setting

else will turn up. I suggest we spend more time investigating."

This is a classic judge vs. perceiver discussion. Who can say who is correct?

The point is, every group will have some opposite personality types. Although this is a source of potential disharmony, it is also a source of potential enrichment. The key is for those serving together to recognize the strengths and limitations of each person's personality type, including their own, and to express appreciation for others' contributions. Understanding personality type theory is wise policy.

7

Growing in Christ through Understanding Personality Type

❖ Throughout the history of the Christian Church, Church leaders have seen it as their responsibility to help other Christians grow to spiritual maturity (see, for example, Ephesians 4:13). We see this reflected all the way back to the days Jesus spent teaching and training His inner circle. It continued as the Church began to grow; the older, more mature Christians took new converts to the faith under their wings. Note how, for example, the apostle Paul discipled the young Timothy in the ways of the Lord. Later, monasteries served as special centers for spiritual development. Individuals would seek out a monk or nun having the reputation for wisdom in these matters. Thus continued the long and glorious tradition of spiritual direction.

Done right, spiritual direction or discipling, as it is sometimes called in evangelical circles, is not so much teaching, counseling or training in ministry—although it does involve aspects of these three things. Rather, it is coaching to help an individual come into spiritual maturity.

Again, the key word is balance. If the spiritual direction is too

Growing in Christ through Understanding Personality Type

broad, the guidance may not adhere to the truths of the Christian faith. Much of what seems liberal or freeing can actually lead into spiritual bondage. If the spiritual direction is too narrow, the guidance given will be of limited value. Far worse is the harm it can do, for such narrowness in spiritual direction could lead those being directed into spiritual frustration—"I've tried and tried this very type of prayer and it just doesn't work"—that they assume God does not love them.

This is, in fact, one of the ways personality can be wounded—by forcing someone into someone else's spiritual framework. If a person thus forced cannot get his or her prayer life on track, it is assumed that he or she is not really trying or is hiding some deep, unconfessed sin. Sometimes these things are true, but it is also possible that the individual has been pressured into a prayer style that fits the pastor or spiritual director. Even though the guidance may be orthodox, it does not fit the one trying to grow.

Balance comes in maintaining the boundaries of biblical truth while celebrating the variety within those boundaries. This will help the searcher find that place most conducive to his or her growth.

I have found helpful that statement written in 1789 in the Preface to the first American Episcopal *Book of Common Prayer*: "It is a most valuable part of that blessed liberty wherewith Christ hath made us free, that in his worship different forms and usages may without offence be allowed, provided the substance of the Faith be kept entire. . . ." There is the balance: *Variety is encouraged, orthodoxy is expected.*

Bishop Phillips Brooks, author of the Christmas carol "O Little Town of Bethlehem," noted in his lectures at Yale University that preaching was "truth through personality." And not just preaching. We might add that one's prayer, worship, belief and ministry must also be truth as seen through that person's personality—God's truth as expressed in the style that is most like him or herself. A personality without truth is not a godly expression. And truth devoid of the personal expression God gave us will be stiff, unenjoyable and seem inauthentic.

As I look over the history of the Church I see the times when she erred on one side or the other—either denying a variety of expression and forcing everyone into a particular mold, or denying the necessity of keeping the substance of the faith entire. In other words, too little variety or too much, too conservative or too liberal, deeming to be absolute that which is only a preference or making the truth itself a variable or an option.

Thanks be to God that the ministry of spiritual direction is making a strong comeback today! Parallel with this is the study of that aspect of theology called spirituality. *Spirituality* might be defined as "the way you express your commitment to Christ."

In general, there are vertical and horizontal dimensions to this commitment. The vertical expression is your growth in relationship to God. The horizontal expression is your growth in relationship to others. Aspects of your relationship to God are prayer, worship and Bible study. Aspects of your relationship to others are evangelism, pastoral care, meeting practical needs and matters of justice. All of these are important and all Christians are called to grow in each of them. Each Christian, however, will express these aspects of discipleship in different ways. Likewise, denominations have corporate spiritual personalities.

Within the boundaries of orthodoxy, the Christians in them may express their relationship to God and others in a rich variety of ways. Wise spiritual direction recognizes this variety and helps individuals find the ways that are best for them within those boundaries.

It may be helpful to see personality type as a different way of being gifted. In the New Testament there are several lists of spiritual gifts (Romans 12:1-8; 1 Corinthians 12:1-12; Ephesians 4:7, 11-12; 1 Peter 4:10-11). Scripture tells us that: (1) Each Christian has one or more of these gifts; (2) we need each other because no one has all the gifts; (3) they are given by God to glorify God, build up the Church and extend the Kingdom, and so on. The same can be said for the diversity of personality: (1) There are different personality types; (2) we need each other because each personality type has insights to give to the others, and, since each personality type has its own weak spots, we need the corrective balancing of others; and (3) we are to glorify God and serve others through the personalities He has given us.

It would be simplistic and wrong to say that a person's personality type automatically points to the particular way he or she expresses Christian discipleship. While it is true that many people who are extraverts better express their faith in a worship style that is energetic and outgoing, some extraverts prefer quiet, introvert worship.

Why is this? Remember, in our discussion of the shadow we noted that some people need to find God in a place within themselves different from that which is used for relating with the world. If God is wholly Other, then perhaps a different part of us is kept for encountering Him. One teenager told me, "I love rock and roll music, but when I worship God, I want the classics. Some of my friends like contemporary Christian rock. They express their faith in God using the style of music that they like all the time. But this doesn't work for me. I find that when I come to God, I need something so different that I know I'm on holy ground."

So, please, if you are in a position of helping an individual grow spiritually, *do not* fall into the trap that is sometimes common in spiritual directors conversant with personality type the-

Free to Be Me!

ory: Don't demand that a person's spirituality style match his or her personality type.

I once witnessed a dear, sweet nun giving this counsel to a woman who came to her for guidance: "According to the Myers-Briggs Type Indicator you are an INFP. Let me give you a handout. It tells you all about INFP spirituality. This is the type of prayer, worship, Bible study and so on that will work for you." Maybe it will. Then again, maybe not. Such advice, though given sincerely, could be harmful if the way that person best relates to God is different from her INFP personality.

Far better would be the comments I heard another nun give: "You came out ESTJ on the Myers-Briggs test. Since the majority of people find their spirituality to match their personality, let's start here. I'm going to give you some projects I'd like you to work on. They are ways of praying, worshiping, studying Scripture and so on that are expressive of an ESTJ personality. Try those for a while. They might prove very helpful to you. Then again, you might find these aren't you at all. We'll talk about it. It could be that you just need more experience in this way of expressing your relationship with God, especially if this was not how you were raised in church. Or it could mean that this style will never be you. If that's the case, we'll try some other things. Eventually we'll find the style that fits you best, at least for now."

She might also make use of Christian biographies, in which you see notable Christians expressing their faith in different styles of spirituality. When you read of quiet contemplatives and busy activists, champions of orthodoxy and lovers of souls, people with ordered devotional lives and unscheduled people like St. Francis, you meet some people like yourself. You grow more confident that you can express your love of the Lord in the way that's right for you style-wise because these heroes of the faith did, too.

Trying a variety of spirituality styles is slower than forcing a person into a mold, but it is wiser. Wiser because not all people fit the personality/spirituality interface mold. Some ENTP people just do not have ENTP spiritualities, however inconvenient and inefficient that might be for their director! It is also wiser because there is no rule that says once we start one style of prayer, Bible study, worship and the like, we can't turn around and try a different path if our original path is no longer helpful.

I believe it is also helpful for God's people to try other styles of spiritual expression besides the one that works best for them, even once this style is found. Why is that?

First of all, because it will help you understand the spiritual styles of other people.

We clergy of St. Paul's Church were all extraverts whose style of worship was also extravert. We enjoyed the ten o'clock service, an extravert service if there ever was one! What we didn't fully understand was the desire of the eight-o'clockers to keep their service quiet and low-key.

"Low-key means they're not really into worship," observed one of us (fortunately, I forget which one!). "Psalm 100:1 tells us to make a joyful noise unto the Lord. Apparently they would rather just sit there as passive spectators." The other two of us agreed. There were a lot of hurt feelings until someone finally convinced us that making the eight o'clock service to be just like the ten o'clock was very unwise and that "Be still, and know that I am God" (Psalm 46:10) is also part of Scripture. As we sample the different kinds of legitimate, orthodox Christian spiritual expressions, we understand our fellow Christians more.

I recommend sampling. It is good to try a few different styles of worship, Christian social action and Bible study from time to

Free to Be Me!

time. Attend a silent retreat, a charismatic prayer meeting, a highly liturgical service, an ethnic service. Help out at a soup kitchen, sit in on a planning meeting of the group that works with the homeless, accompany someone who is going to talk with political leaders. Participate in a highly structured, intellectual Bible study and an informal sharing group. Once or twice a year be part of something that is not the usual way you express your faith. You don't have to go back regularly if you don't wish, but you will learn a lot about your brothers and sisters in Christ for having attended.

If you are in leadership, you must work at this sampling process to ensure that these various spiritual expressions of the faith are accessible. If it is not possible to have them available in your church, try to let the people know who else offers them in your area.

Some in the church growth movement argue that a particular congregation should not try to be all things to all people. Instead, a particular church should try to be good at just one or two things, with the understanding that other churches can minister to other types. There is some validity to that idea. But what if a husband needs one type of spiritual expression and the wife another? Or the parents one type and the children another? While it might be somewhat inconvenient for people to attend different prayer meetings, worship services or study sessions in the same church to find that which is most conducive to spiritual growth, should it be necessary to attend different churches?

Second, while you may be more one kind of personality than another, seldom is this to the extreme.

That is to say, while you may be clearly an extravert, few if any are so extravertish that there is no introvert part to them at all. This is true in terms of spirituality as well. While you might like extravertish worship most of the time, you may need a quiet, introvert service on occasion. Why not have a variety within the same congregation so that the occasional need for something other than what a person normally likes is met?

Third, people sometimes change with age.

Clinical psychologists and theoreticians in personality type theory state that as a person gets older there is sometimes a change, occasionally pronounced, in his or her personality type as the shadow side emerges. For a few people, what had been the shadow may become the dominant personality. If you are at home in a particular congregation and then undergo this change in personality type, must you leave that congregation, or are there other expressions of the faith in that same church for you?

I knew charismatics who, as they got older, stopped attending their charismatic prayer groups and, instead, attended quiet, early morning midweek services. While in a few cases it was because they turned away from the gifts of the Spirit, for most of them it was just a matter of change in personality. Marianne put it this way: "I still make use of the gifts of the Spirit as much as ever. It's just that I need to express my love for God in a quieter way now."

On the other hand, I saw three ever-so-proper ladies in their late fifties, each one the model of a traditional Episcopalian, start attending their church's charismatic prayer meeting. One of them put it like this: "What I was before was good for me then. This is right for me now."

What got them to try it in the first place? I had suggested to that congregation, some years before, that once a year everyone should try a worship service or study group that was different from what they were used to or preferred. They wouldn't have to go back for another year unless they wanted to, but they did need to go once.

One person who caught the importance of my request called it "Trying something different to see how other members of the church worship." "Spiritual slumming" was the description of somebody obedient to but not exactly with the program. At any rate, those women attended the midweek prayer and praise service once a year instead of their quiet midweek Communion service.

On Sundays they preferred the quiet eight o'clock service to the more high-powered ten o'clock family service. But then they noticed, as one of them put it, "It wasn't doing anything for us anymore. When we went out for coffee afterward we found ourselves wondering why everything was so sluggish."

"You don't suspect," another one of them suggested, "that we're becoming more, dare I say it, ten o'clockish, do you?"

As they later related to me, "We found out, ten o'clockish nothing! We were turning into Friday night prayer and praise people. Imagine!"

I often wonder what would have happened had their church not offered both a quiet midweek Communion and a noisy midweek prayer and praise service, and had they not accepted my challenge. Would those women have discovered the service that they now need to help them grow? My guess is no. And they would probably have stopped growing spiritually, remaining faithful as Christians but wondering why their spiritual growth had ceased.

Let's take a look at each of the personality types and see how they relate to seven aspects of spirituality—prayer, worship, Bible study, evangelism, pastoral care, meeting practical needs and issues of justice.

I will use the term *spiritual* before the personality type ("spiritual extravert," etc.) to remind us that this is a description of that kind of spirituality whether or not the person using it is that personality type. In other words, spiritual extravert describes what the particular aspect of spirituality is like in an extravert form. The person expressing it may or may not be an extravert.

Failure to recognize this may cause people to be wounded, something we are trying to overcome.

Extravert/Introvert Spirituality

Extravert spirituality can be described as energetic and outgoing. Representative Scriptures could be, "Praise him with the clash of cymbals!" (Psalm 150:5). "They were all together in one place" (Acts 2:1).

Introvert spirituality can be described as quiet and individual. Operative Scriptures could be, "The Lord is in his holy temple; let all the earth be silent before him" (Habakkuk 2:20). "Jesus went off to a quiet place to pray" (Matthew 14:23; Mark 1:35, 6:46; Luke 6:12; etc.).

In terms of prayer, spiritual extraverts prefer praying in a group to praying individually. Such a prayer group may have a set prayer list, from which each person prays out loud (judges, with their sense of order, may appreciate this), or else the members may pray out loud spontaneously as they feel moved (something that may appeal more to the spontaneity of a perceiver). Spiritual extraverts like unison prayers, where many are praying the same prayer together.

Even when praying silently, spiritual extraverts would rather pray with others around than alone. For that reason many spiritual extraverts would rather go to church fifteen minutes early to pray while others are assembling for worship than spend those fifteen minutes alone in a prayer closet. While it is possible that spiritual extraverts may become so dependent on others that their own individual spiritual lives are neglected, they represent the Body of Christ coming before the Lord in unified worship.

Spiritual introverts prefer to pray quietly. They like a place far from other people and distractions. If they pray at church, they

Free to Be Me!

would rather pray quietly by themselves, separated from other people, if possible. If they are with other people and are asked to pray out loud, they prefer that both the volume and energy level of the people present be low. While spiritual introverts may be so comfortable with praying alone that they stand aloof from other members of the Body of Christ, still they remind us that God has no nephews and nieces, only sons and daughters, and that on the Judgment Day we stand before the Lord as individuals.

In terms of worship, there is no question what kind the spiritual extraverts prefer: Worship with large numbers of people present, lots of activity, a high level of energy and excitement, stimulating music and so on. Interaction between people is appreciated—whether personally in the Exchange of the Peace with others or vicariously as the worship leader shares informally, perhaps humorously, the announcements of the day.

Spiritual introverts would rather that worship be quieter. Many spiritual introverts prefer to worship God by themselves. When they worship with others, they prefer things quiet and gentle. One person told me why she liked the early service at her church: "No kids, no music, not many people." It wasn't that this woman disliked people. She liked them very much. But when she worshiped she wanted to be lost in quiet reverence with the focus on God. Several spiritual introverts have complained to me about clergy who interject too much of themselves into the service: "It takes the focus off God and puts it onto a person."

I have already mentioned our ten o'clock service at St. Paul's Church in Malden. It was loud, energetic and long—usually around two hours. About halfway through the service we came to the part of the liturgy called the Exchange of the Peace. The person leading the service would say to the congregation, "The peace of the Lord be always with you." The congregation would then respond, "And also with you." Then, as in most churches, people would spend a few minutes greeting the people around them.

About twenty years ago, the Exchange of the Peace was restored to the liturgy of many churches to demonstrate that we must first be reconciled with one another before we can offer our gift to the Lord or receive His body and blood. The Exchange of the Peace is also in the liturgy to remind us that worship is the activity of the Body of Christ, not just the private affair of individuals.

While this speaks equally to both extraverts and introverts, there is a reason extraverts prefer it: It is a chance for fellowship, for a time of socializing in the midst of the service. In many churches, the people are taught that sharing the peace of the Lord with one another reminds us of the corporate nature of the Church. In other churches, however, it is basically a time for fellowship. As such it is often barely tolerated by introverts who prefer to leave that sort of thing for the coffee hour.

I started noticing in Malden that at a certain point more than an hour into the service, several of our ten o'clock parishioners ran to the bathrooms. I had assumed this was because they had been in church for more than an hour and just needed to go. After some months I noticed that it was always the same persons rushing out. Did these individuals have bladder problems? I was wondering aloud about this with a perceptive person who, incidentally, had taken my personality type and personal growth workshop.

"No, Mark, that isn't it at all," he responded. "They're introverts running for cover before the Exchange of the Peace begins." Then I thought about it some more. In Malden, sharing the peace was industrial-strength! It was high-energy and lasted about ten minutes. No wonder these poor spiritual introverts fled.

Free to Be Me!

To them this manner of Exchanging the Peace was Killer Peace, a name I used for it thereafter!

It was also interesting to me that certain children could behave for the two-hour duration of that service who I knew could not last through the hour-long service in their previous church. I asked one young couple about that because it didn't make sense to me.

"Oh, we understand," one of them shared. "In our former church, the service was so quiet and formal that any movement or wiggle would disrupt the mood. Here at St. Paul's everybody is wiggling all the time! Billy fits in perfectly. His coloring or reading or looking around doesn't disrupt. Plus the service is high-energy and it makes Billy feel church is friendly. In our former church, he couldn't relate himself to worship at all."

Since that time, I have thought about many young people who became church dropouts as soon as they could stand up to their parents. In many cases, the parents were introverts (or mild extraverts) who preferred a quiet service, while their youngsters were extraverts who needed—but were not given—a worship service where they could express their energy. The reverse problem also exists, of course, but in my experience it manifests itself differently. The introvert growing up in an extravert church does not usually gravitate to a quiet worship service until young adulthood; by that time the extravert, growing up in an introvert church, is long gone.

Bible study is also done in different ways depending on spiritual personality. Spiritual extraverts prefer group study with lots of opportunity for discussion and sharing. As extraverts' favorite realm is the world, they like to learn about God by examining God's acts in history. Spiritual introverts prefer to study by themselves, or, if in a group, prefer a lecture. As their preferred realm is the inner world of the mind, their way of knowing about

God is through ideas or through an intensely personal experience. If the extravert knows God through the earthquake, wind and fire of His mighty acts, the introvert knows Him, as did Elijah, through a still, small voice.

If there are differences in the way we express the vertical relationship to God, there are also differences in the way we express the horizontal relationship to others.

Regarding evangelism, a certain church had just finished giving a spiritual gifts inventory test, a questionnaire designed to help people discover which of the various spiritual gifts they have and their role in God's Kingdom.

Several people tested out high in this area of evangelism. The pastor invited them to a meeting in his study one evening to give them some basic training in how to share the faith. The pastor, himself a successful evangelist, started explaining how to go up to strangers on the street, how to visit homes in a neighborhood, how to hand booklets to the bus driver and so on. While the spiritual extraverts found this helpful and looked forward to going out and witnessing with their pastor, the spiritual introverts present found this to be very anxiety-provoking. A few expressed great reservation about ever doing any of those things. They were encouraged to trust the Lord and do it anyway. A few of them did and found themselves to be so anxious and upset that they quit evangelizing.

This caused the group a good deal of confusion. What went wrong? These people had tested high in evangelism. Was the test seriously flawed? It seemed in many ways to be a good indicator of what gifts people possessed. Were these people lazy or spiritually rebellious? That did not seem to be the case either.

The problem was that they did not realize it is not enough just to understand spiritual gifts: It is important to understand spiritual gifts in the context of personality type. That is to say, anyone who has a regular ministry of evangelism should have that spiritual gift, but *how* he or she exercises that ministry is dependent on personality type.

Simply put, extraverts evangelize differently from introverts. Extraverts can be more realistically expected to approach strangers, visit in the homes of people they have never met, talk in front of groups and so on. Introverts will evangelize more quietly, often with people to whom they have already been introduced, and in a much more low-key manner. This does not make one better than the other. In fact, some people, turned off to one style, can probably be reached only by somebody of the opposite personality.

Let me make a strong plea to those churches using any of the various personality type instruments to be careful with how you use the results. As you teach people how to minister according to the spiritual gifts the instruments indicate, take their personality types into account. Otherwise, the result could be frustration, anger, a false sense of guilt and a feeling that they cannot be used in God's service.

While we may readily understand that an individual's personality determines the way his or her spiritual gifts are used, we might also wonder if God bestows particular spiritual gifts on certain personality types. Some interesting work is going on at Andrews University that has demonstrated empirically specific correlations between a person's personality and the cluster of gifts the Holy Spirit has given him or her. (If you are interested, you might write to Dr. Roy C. Naden, Professor of Religious Education, Andrews University, Berrien Springs, MI 49104.)

Pastoral care is also a function of spiritual personality type. Spiritual extraverts will often be out front while spiritual introverts will often work behind the scenes. For seven years, my home church, St. Paul's Episcopal Church in Malden, Massachusetts, distinguished itself, among other ways, for its Bread of Life ministry to the poor and the street people. This ministry happened to shift into high gear about the time I started learning about personality type theory. As a people-watcher I was fascinated to see how true the theory was in terms of who self-selected what kind of job in the feeding ministry. The spiritual extraverts, true to form, were the ones at the serving window and out talking with those who came for dinner. They would sit down at the tables and get to know the people as people. The spiritual introverts, as a rule, tended to stay in the background, working hard at cooking or pot-washing.

There were, of course, exceptions to this. I asked one of our more introverted members how she could sit down and strike up conversations with our guests. "It's difficult," she said, "but it needs to be done. We want these people to know we care about them. We're not just do-gooders handing out food to make ourselves feel good. I *do* care for them. It's difficult for me to get to know people but I swallow my reticence and sit down with them anyway."

We can appreciate the truth in the personality type theory, however, when we compare those remarks with those of one of the extraverts. "How can I sit down with them? Easy. I love to be around people. When the doors open, I think to myself, *Oh, boy! People!*"

Perhaps we should take this opportunity to remind ourselves that the people to whom we minister have personalities, too, and many of them, especially the introverts, may be overwhelmed by an extravert's style of ministry. It is far more Christlike to change our style of ministry depending on the personality of those to whom we are ministering than it is for us to minister the way we like best, regardless of how this affects others. Christian ministry is done for the glory of God, the building up of the Body of Christ and the extension of God's Kingdom, not because it makes us feel good or fulfilled.

Another way in which spiritual extraverts and introverts are different in giving pastoral care has to do with whether they minister in a team or individually. Spiritual extraverts, as a rule, will give pastoral care as part of a team effort while spiritual introverts minister individually. I saw this demonstrated graphically after church one Sunday in the lay Eucharistic ministers, those people who serve Communion to the shut-ins and hospitalized of the parish. One of them, a strong extravert, spent time looking for someone to go along with him, while the introverts quietly slipped out the back door to make their visits by themselves.

The meeting of practical needs is another important ministry. By this I mean such things as driving someone to a doctor's appointment, assisting with emergency housing after a fire, preparing food or cleaning the house for someone who is ill, looking after a youngster to give Mom a morning off. In this ministry we also see how personality type influences function. Spiritual extraverts tend to be part of teams and work publicly. Spiritual introverts tend to work individually (or with a close friend) and behind the scenes.

Matters of justice are much the same. A spiritual extravert is more likely to be vocal, to be part of a group if not actually at the front of the group, to speak up at meetings and so on. A spiritual introvert is more likely to work behind the scenes, write letters and, if in a group, stay in the background.

Sensate/Intuitive Spirituality

A spiritual sensate tends to be more concrete, literal and specific. The focus is the things of the moment, understood in a straightforward way. A spiritual sensate understands the doctrines and duties of the faith in a matter-of-fact way. The focus is the duties of today. His or her Scripture might be, "This is the day the Lord has made; let us rejoice and be glad in it" (Psalm 118:24).

A spiritual intuitive tends to take an expansive view of things. Take anything specific—a point in the liturgy, a specific Bible passage, a doctrine, whatever is happening at the moment—and he or she will use this as the jumping-off point for speculation, imagination, a search for possibilities, meanings, interpretations and applications. Fantasy, imagery and parable all intrigue the spiritual intuitive, while literal, precise definitions often leave him or her unmoved. His or her focus is on the future, stretching forward to see what God might bring or how everything will come together at the end of time. The spiritual intuitive would give hearty assent to the Scripture "Where there is no vision, the people perish" (Proverbs 29:18, KJV).

At prayer, spiritual sensates tend to focus more on specific prayer requests. They tend to like prayer lists and don't find them confining. Specific prayer exercises, that is to say, models of prayer or ways to go about praying, are sometimes helpful, especially to sensates who are also judges. A spiritual sensate prefers that devotional objects—paintings and stained glass windows, for instance—picture a specific event. A spiritual intuitive generally prefers something abstract and symbolic to stimulate a mystical encounter with God. When a spiritual sensate has an encounter with God in prayer, it tends to be matter of fact: "I spoke to Jesus and told Him thus-and-so, and this is what He said to me." A spiritual sensate may need to be encouraged to move from the matter of fact in prayer into something more mystical. Buy him or her a set of wings!

A spiritual intuitive at prayer is very different. Lists can often be confining, especially if the intuitive is a perceiver or not a very strong judge. Often a spiritual intuitive will start praying and go on to another topic, which then suggests another topic and so on. Some people worry about these distractions, but wise spiritual counselors over the centuries have suggested that one turn these distractions into prayer concerns. They pop up, so the advice runs, because the mind suggests them for remembering before God.

Devotional objects tend to be seen as symbols, leading to spiritual truths behind the surface story. In turn, these spiritual truths become prayer topics, which then suggest other topics. A spiritual intuitive's personal encounter with God can be quite mystical. Like the apostle Paul, his or her encounter with God may be inexpressible (2 Corinthians 12:4). If the spiritual intuitive is also a feeler, mystical prayer can be like the experience of falling in love—a sense of warmth deep within that is far deeper than the ability to express or even comprehend. Or, if the spiritual intuitive is also a thinker, the encounter with God is more intellectual—a sense of being caught up in a truth so vast and so deep that one is wonderfully overwhelmed by the vastness of the all-knowing Mind. A spiritual intuitive may need to test the content of the encounter to make sure it squares with reality as revealed to us in Scripture. Buy him or her an anchor!

In worship, a spiritual sensate tends to be matter of fact, as in his or her prayer life. It should be simple and done right. Worship need not be ornate or fancy. "We sing a couple of songs, have a Bible reading, a pastoral prayer, a basic sermon about what a doctrine means or what we're supposed to do or not do, take up a collection, sing another hymn and home we go," was how an elderly man described to me his Congregational church's Sunday service.

Among Roman Catholics, spiritual sensates often desire to

have a simple mass, receive Communion and go on one's way. They often resist ornate, fancy, solemn High Mass, with its mystery and majesty. A spiritual sensate sometimes needs to be reminded that it may be stretching matters to call his a-hymn-a-prayer-a-sermon-and-home-we-go Sunday experience a service of worship. It might be a Bible lecture with a bit of music thrown in, but it doesn't seem to be what the book of Revelation describes as heavenly worship.

And yet, there is something helpful here for those of us who expect a service to be a rapturous encounter with God in our minds or hearts. There are days when we just cannot experience that. Sometimes this is because we are tired, or unwell, or emotionally low, or just having a down day spiritually. Sensates remind us that God meets us nevertheless.

That is why I like that rich balance—again, there's that important word—of the words of administration in the historic Anglican (Episcopal) Communion liturgy. The one administering the bread says: "The Body of our Lord Jesus Christ, which was given for thee, preserve thy body and soul unto everlasting life. Take and eat this in remembrance that Christ died for thee, and feed on him in thy heart by faith with thanksgiving."

I usually focus on the second sentence, the part that is *subjective*. As an intuitive I enjoy stretching my mind to remember the events of Calvary. I examine the state of my faith and yield it up to the Lord for deepening as I feed on Him in my heart. But on those days when I just cannot summon up the effort, or when my faith is weak, what an assurance to know there is also an *objective* part to the sacrament. When I hear "The Body of Christ which was given for thee," I am being told that God is doing something for me apart from my efforts in spiritual growth, my depths of faith or my level of thanksgiving.

It was a sensate, with his simple faith that God was meeting

Free to Be Me!

him in the Sacrament, who reminded me during a time of spiritual befuddlement, "Just take it, Mark. It's good for you."

Worship is simple and straightforward for the spiritual sensate. Not so for the intuitive! Spiritually intuitive Protestants are rediscovering mystery and symbolism. They are designing banners, making their clergy fancy vestments, letting worship lift them past the literal thought and present moment to something more grand and cosmic. In many churches the worship is moving from the simplicity described above to something more liturgical. Spiritually intuitive Roman Catholics look hard for liturgy that has the rich symbolic trappings of the ages, and lament when it is not to be found.

Spiritual intuitives want their worship not only to instruct the fact-oriented left brain but also affect the creative right brain. They don't just want to be taught, they want to be inspired. A spiritual intuitive may need to be reminded that too much warm, mystical heat without the clear light of Gospel truth may entertain, sometimes quite profoundly, but it may not be specifically Christian.

And yet intuitives show us that God wants us to do more than know a few facts about Him or just go quietly about our duties— God wants us to encounter Him. Regarding Communion, they remind us that unless we receive the elements by remembering what Christ did for us and offering ourselves anew to Him in faith, we may be looking on it as magic.

Monsignor Chester Michael echoes the correctives at work in Roman Catholicism that seek to move that church from too much stress on the externals of the sacrament to a position more balanced. He writes, "When the sacraments are used as authentic, living religious symbols, they retain the presence of mystery, awe, and reverence toward a power that we do not fully understand and cannot control. Through the use of living religious symbols (and the seven sacraments are such symbols!), we are aware of being in the presence of tremendous, mysterious, awesome, yet fascinating and attractive, transcendent powers which we are unable to control as we might arbitrarily choose."*

Bible study is not only done differently by spiritually sensate and intuitive persons; it carries some profound opportunities if done correctly and serious dangers if not.

Spiritually sensate persons generally approach Bible study with an attitude of "Read it and believe what it says and do what it asks." And why not? God does not play games with us, asking us to take out our secret decoder rings to figure out what He *actually* meant behind what is written. Being literal, the spiritually sensate person knows this well.

"When the Bible says for us not to do something, what word is in code?" These were the words of a man angered by his denomination's vote no longer to consider a certain moral offense as sin. Spiritual sensates know that while some parts of Scripture are symbolic, other parts are not. "Moses did not come down the mountain with the Ten Suggestions," a bishop once told me.

Whether by force of habit or to get out of doing what God has decreed, intuitives sometimes wish to find symbol and hidden meaning where there is none. "Well, it depends on what it means" is a phrase often used by someone who really means, "I know darn well what it means but I don't want to do it. But I'm more sophisticated than to say that, so I will obfuscate by using theological language, invoking the concepts of parable, religious myth and so on."

Mark Twain was once asked if he had trouble with the parts of

* From *The Open Door*, volume IV, number 4, 1985. *The Open Door* is published quarterly by Msgr. Michael Publishers. It contains a wealth of insight into the spiritual life with special reference to personality type. For further information write him at P.O. Box 855, Charlottesville, VA 22902.

Free to Be Me!

the Bible he didn't understand. "No," he responded, "I have trouble with the parts of the Bible I *do* understand." Twain, unlike some spiritual intuitives, was honest enough to admit that much of the Bible is rather straightforward and we do not always like what God is telling us to do! The insight of the spiritual sensate can bring a much-needed corrective.

A spiritual sensate will also often give careful attention to detail. He or she will sometimes employ maps, Bible dictionaries, concordances and commentaries to get the precise, complete meaning. When he prepares a Bible study it is not enough just to grab a few verses and start speculating; he wants to look up all the relevant verses so as to get the full teaching of Scripture on the subject.

One college student told me of the importance of the thorough research she had done in preparation for a class she was teaching: "If you grab just a few verses in James you might get the impression that we are saved by our good works. If you grab just a few verses from Romans you might think good works don't matter at all. But when you research the matter thoroughly, you find one comprehensive New Testament doctrine on faith and works, with the different New Testament writers each examining the issue from a different angle. I put a lot of work into this, but it was worth it. Otherwise, we might draw an unbalanced conclusion."

Sensates ask precise questions. "Where, exactly, did Paul go next? Wasn't it Malchus who lost an ear to Peter's sword? What is the best translation of those key words in the Beatitudes? Of what significance is it that those shepherds watched their flocks *at night*?" And they expect correct, precise answers. If one is not available, they do not want speculation or fanciful theories, especially if they obscure the clear and simple meaning of the text. As a result, spiritual sensates often have trouble in Bible studies with spiritual intuitives: "They seem to be so off into their theories that they miss what is right in front of them."

Meanwhile, the spiritual intuitives are having trouble with the spiritual sensates: "They are so pedantic and literal-minded, they probably think that when Jesus said He was the door, He wanted us to believe He was literally made of wood." Similarly, C. S. Lewis commented that when Jesus told us to be like doves, He didn't mean for us to lay eggs! The spiritual intuitives let their creative minds search for the rich, deep, poetic symbolism of Scripture. They know that the letter kills but the Spirit gives life (2 Corinthians 3:6), so they ask, "Why just settle for what is on the page when there is so much more behind it?"

Spiritual intuitives know that their gift of seeing the possibilities helps them apply the truths of Scripture to a whole variety of changing circumstances. I was once at a Bible study where the discussion topic was, "When Scripture asks us to work for justice, what might this mean?" I wasn't surprised when the intuitives were the ones who made most of the suggestions. The sensates in the room were better at quoting what Jesus and the Old Testament prophets had actually said, but were not as good as the intuitives at speculating as to what could be done differently in the world today.

Spiritual intuitives note that sometimes one can so focus on the precise words that one misses the bigger picture. They point to Jesus' rebuke of the Pharisees for being so bound up in the minute details of tithing (the mint and dill and cummin) that they neglected law, justice, mercy and faith (Matthew 23:23). What the spiritual intuitives forget, however, is that Jesus did not say the Pharisees were wrong to tithe in this way, but that they were wrong to neglect the weightier matters of the Law while going about doing their precise tithing. The danger in moving past the literal to get to the deeper meaning is that in doing so one often loses both.

Spiritual intuitives, often disliking the slog of slow, painful, *detailed* research, may move past it for creative interpretations. They love to think about what symbols symbolize. Leave the Gospel of Mark with its regular, predictable recitation of events and speeches to the spiritual sensates. The spiritual intuitives love the Gospel of John because there are enough abstract words and concepts to chew on indefinitely! They note that Jesus often spoke in parables, and we profit not from the specific details but the theological or ethical point of the story, which we then have to apply to today. That takes more than just looking things up in a Bible dictionary or on a map; it takes interpretation and application.

A wise Bible leader should make sure that both the actual statements of Scripture with its doctrinal and ethical teaching are understood and accepted and that the deeper nuances of those broad, abstract words are given full justice. Approached correctly, those two things are not in conflict. The Bible is simple but not simplistic. Its teachings can be understood by children and its depth can never be fully fathomed by the greatest philosophers. It gives us common sense guidance for daily life and ever stretches our minds and spirits. *Its teachings may be more than literal, but they are never less than literal.* It often means much more than what it first appears to be saying, but never less than its plain and simple meaning. It points to the fact that while the Truth is fixed (something the sensate champions), it applies to a world that is always changing (something to which an intuitive may be more attuned.) Wise is the Bible student who, regardless of spiritual personality type, knows these things.

In evangelism spiritual sensates and spiritual intuitives tend to work in different ways. Sensates tend to like such methodical, straightforward presentations of the Gospel as the Four Spiritual

Laws or the two basic questions of Evangelism Explosion. They want to present the basic facts of the Gospel without a lot of frills.

The strength in this is that it is, indeed, the Gospel that is presented, not a lot of religious side issues. Another advantage is that the person hearing this presentation is not confused. The outline is simple. He or she is responding to the basic message and is not sidetracked into secondary issues. The danger is that the presentation may come off as a canned speech. Further, what if the ones being evangelized have important questions that lie outside the basic outline? Can the evangelist deal with those, or does departing from the outline lead to confusion? And, finally, there can be the danger, especially with sensates who are also judges, that the evangelizers are so eager to run through the outline of the Gospel that a person is pressured into making a decision before he or she is ready.

Spiritual intuitives have the opposite strengths and weaknesses. They often share the Gospel in less of a detailed, precise outline form. As a result, they are free to go wherever the conversation goes or the Spirit leads, answering questions that the person being evangelized actually wants to address and showing the breadth and depth of the Christian message. The advantage is that the conversation does not look like a canned speech. If the person being evangelized has previously been approached by others sharing their message and has been turned off to what is obviously a memorized talk, he or she might find the approach of the spiritual intuitive refreshing.

There are dangers, though. In the conversation, did the spiritual intuitive actually get around to stating, however circuitously, the basics of the Gospel message? As we read the epistles and examine their speeches in the book of Acts we find that the New Testament leaders, no matter what the styles or personalities, always shared certain basic, core points.

Free to Be Me!

Spiritual intuitives who are also perceivers need to be especially careful that the conversation does not just ramble about aimlessly. There is a time to say to a person, "Would you like to accept Jesus as your Lord and Savior?" Sometimes intuitives do not always reach that point.

Pastoral care is often done differently according to spiritual personality. As spiritual sensates are more attuned to specific detail, they are often the ones who remember a widow who is usually depressed on the anniversary of her husband's death and what it is that helps her. They are the ones, especially if they are also feelers, who routinely visit the hospitals and nursing homes, bringing a comb to this person, or a magazine to that one, because they recalled those were requested at their last visit.

A spiritual intuitive will not usually be so detail-oriented. In fact, he or she will often forget these specific things and, if also a thinker (as opposed to feeler), will not understand why this inattention to detail may hurt some people's feelings. But he or she may come up with some very good ideas as to how a church's pastoral care ministry may be conducted.

"Why don't we get the youth group to visit the nursing homes?" Greta suggested one day. "And also the Scout troop. The youth group leader is teaching a unit on the elderly and the Scout troop has to have service projects. We can stagger their visits so the folks aren't overwhelmed one month and then left alone for months afterward. The Men's Service Club seems a bit bored lately and all the fix-it jobs around here are completed. Maybe they could visit our men in the nursing home or hospital occasionally and share stories and run errands."

"Great idea, Greta," was the response. "Will you head this up?"

"Absolutely not!" Greta replied. "I've learned that my gift to the Body of Christ is to be the idea woman. You know what happens when I'm put in charge of the work. Details choke me! I'm not shirking responsibility. I'll work as hard as anyone else, but in the follow-through, as a teammate of some detail person. No, let me stay in my role as idea generator. We need to get a detail and organization person to run this." (This detail and organization person would most likely be a sensate-judge.)

When it comes to the meeting of practical needs, you can probably guess that the sensates will carry the load. Intuitives generally do not have the gift for this. That is not to say there isn't the occasional sensate who doesn't follow through or the occasional intuitive who can work with detail, but these people are the exceptions.

In matters of justice, predictably, the sensates are attuned to specific issues while intuitives are aware of the larger picture. I saw this demonstrated graphically in a group of people I knew. I had previously given most of them my Myers-Briggs workshop so I wanted to see if they responded true to type when confronting the needs of street people. Nearly all the sensates responded to the problem by working out specific responses to the needs of individuals. This man needed a home; that family could be sheltered by relatives but they had to be transported to New Jersey; this woman could do unskilled labor but needed to get an infection cleared up first; this teenager wanted to get his life turned around but needed tutoring. The sensates responded to each case as it came along, found the specific needs that each person had and responded accordingly in a step-by-step, practical way.

The intuitives, as could be expected, were not as good at that kind of detailed, individual response. What grabbed them immediately was the larger picture: Why, in this land of relative affluence, was there homelessness in the first place? Did "the system" make it more advantageous for a single-parent family to get help than a family that was intact? Was it rent control that

Free to Be Me!

stabilized prices for those fortunate enough to rent but destroyed any incentive for additional homes to be built? Was it allowing cheap foreign goods to flood the country that dried up jobs for semi-skilled labor? Was it the declining moral values that destigmatized illegitimacy? Was it individual, corporate and government greed and misplaced priorities? Was it the indifference of those mainline churches that talked the talk of caring and passed resolutions but never actually got down to doing anything about the problem?

Having thought about the possible causes of the problem, they started considering what courses of action could be taken. Picketing? Letter-writing? Media blitz? Organizing local churches? Getting the support of those politicians who might be predisposed to help and turning up the heat on those who might not be?

Sure enough, this group of people responded true to type with the sensates ministering to specific issues and the intuitives looking at the big picture. We need both approaches. If the Church were all sensates, they would be busy fixing the problems but seldom addressing the causes of those problems. Left unaddressed, there would continue to be a steady, if not overwhelming, supply of people needing to be helped. If there were just intuitives there might be some worthy action taken at the source of the problem, but the individuals with needs might be left unhelped.

Thinker/Feeler Spirituality

It has been my experience that the area of spiritual thinker-feeler is the one in which we most see people expressing their faith in ways opposite from their everyday personalities. (We also see this with the extravert-introvert personality pair, but not nearly as much as we do with the spiritual thinker-feeler function).

Often the person who normally relates to others as thinker is enraptured with feelings when it comes to God. A few of these people have told me that they would think it promiscuous to feel so intimate with anyone other than God. Others have said that it is only God whom they will let into the deepest part of their hearts.

On the other hand, some feelers have told me that their feelings, all warm and mushy, may be nice for people but, as one big old teddy bear of a construction worker told me, "When it comes to God, you take your hat off and kneel before the King of the universe. Oh, He's my friend, all right, but no way is He my pal." So remember, we are talking in this chapter about *spiritual* personality, which may or may not be the same as one's personality otherwise.

At prayer, a spiritual thinker will more likely contemplate the attributes of God—His omnipotent power, His omniscient wisdom, His eternal agelessness, His self-giving love and so on. To have one's mind contemplate God is to be caught up in the pure and complete truth that God is. Thus, prayer for a spiritual thinker often includes contemplation of God—in a more matter-of-fact way for one who is also a spiritual sensate, or in a more speculative way for one who is also a spiritual intuitive.

Spiritual thinkers often meditate in prayer on doctrinal truths, the Trinity, for example, and then let their confession of sin, intercessions and petitions follow accordingly. Prayer of adoration is often standing in awe of the truth in its pureness and clarity more than it is devotion to the Person of God. The danger, of course, is that the God of the Bible, active in history, the lover of souls, becomes a religious abstraction, like the Unmoved Mover of Greek religious philosophy.

Free to Be Me!

Spiritual feelers may do little or none of this. For them, prayer is the chance to spend time with their heavenly Friend. For them knowing *about* God may be interesting intellectually, but knowing God *personally* is even better. (By the way, the spiritual thinker would protest this statement and say, "Knowing *about* someone is not mere intellectualism. It is a true and real way to know someone.")

Prayer for the spiritual feeler is simply basking in the joy of being present with God. Sharing hurts, needs, frustrations and sins is not so much a formal presentation to the King as it is talking things over with one's best Friend. Contemplation of truth does not interest a spiritual feeler very much, but adoration of God does. The word *devotions* aptly describes a feeler's prayers.

The danger is that God can be so enjoyed as Friend that He ceases to be respected as the Lord of the universe or that the spiritual feeler bases his or her understanding of truth on subjective perceptions. The former can lead to a sentimentality that makes it difficult to trust God for powerful intervention as righteous Judge. The latter can make religion seem like something out of *Alice in Wonderland*—I can make God be whatever I want God to be. It can also lead to a "taming" of God where we invite Him to make us feel good but where we neither stand in fear of Him nor seek His glory above all else.

This sentimentalizing of God can occur on both ends of the political/intellectual/religious spectrum. I have seen conservative pietists enjoy their cozy, holy huddle, warm and safe with their sweet Jesus while abysmal human suffering was occurring all around them. When one man told me, "All He wants is our love," he obviously meant love as restricted to emotions. My response was, "No, He also wants our activity on behalf of the least in our world." I have also seen liberal activists relate to Jesus as their comrade-in-arms on a crusade to rid the world of this or that vice. By being on the march with Jesus, they felt sufficiently excused from either obeying Him in their sexual behavior or worshiping Him with their hearts. In either case, the personal relationship with God was seen as warrant to ignore the more troublesome parts of God's will for His disciples, however a particular person may define *troublesome*.

Two theological terms—*transcendent* and *immanent*—are appropriately noted here. Being transcendent, God is high, mighty and lofty. This does not mean that He disappears from any relationship with His children, but rather that He is exalted above all of the earth, over which He exercises divine control. Generally speaking, spiritual thinkers (especially if they are also introverts) relate well to God's transcendence and believe that things are out of control and God's honor is sullied if He is too much down here.

Spiritual feelers (especially if they are also extraverts) relate better to the immanence of God. Yes, they know God is lofty, majestic and all that. But more important, He is right here with me, comforting and strengthening me, and walking the lonely and troublesome roads of life with me. If a spiritual feeler does not feel God's close presence, His lofty majesty might as well be a void in the heavens.

In worship, a spiritual thinker likes hymns that speak about the truths of the faith, for example, "Immortal, invisible, God only wise, in light inaccessible hid from our eyes . . ." or "Holy, holy, holy! Lord God Almighty! . . . God in three Persons, blessed Trinity." Spiritual feelers like hymns that express their personal relationship with God, for example, "What a Friend we have in Jesus!" or "He walks with me and He talks with me, and He tells me I am His own."

In worship, a spiritual thinker likes an atmosphere conducive to thinking and contemplating. While this is mitigated somewhat

Free to Be Me!

for spiritual *extravert*-thinkers, it is heightened for spiritual *introvert*-thinkers. For the spiritual thinker, the hymns, prayers, sermon and worship atmosphere all are evaluated on the basis of how well they minister to the mind. "I like our new pastor," George said. "He gives me something to chew on all week."

A spiritual feeler, on the other hand, wants warmth. "Christ Church is such a cold church," Beverly noted. What she wanted from Sunday worship was a sense of friendship and fellowship among the members and with God. Spiritual feelers are the first to sense tension in a church and find it a barrier to worship.

As an organist, I like to examine new hymnals when they first come out. Part of the criteria with which I rate them is whether they are sufficiently narrow and sufficiently broad. In other words: If it expresses a desire to be all things to all people, is the objective truth of the Gospel sacrificed for the sake of (false) inclusivity? And, conversely: Within the bounds of the truth, are all the various spiritual personality types well accommodated?

As an Episcopalian, I am most familiar with the hymnal of our denomination, *The Hymnal 1982*. The commission charged with preparing the book looked for theological orthodoxy, poetic beauty and integrity of meaning (from the book's Preface)—a good thinker activity. They acted as feelers, however, in making sensitive alteration of texts that could be interpreted as either pejorative or discriminatory. In addition, to reflect the pluralistic nature of the Church, hymns were selected from Native American, Afro-American, Hispanic and Asian sources.

As far as all of this goes, the commission did a fine job, producing—in one sense—a culturally more comprehensive book. What they were blind to, however, was the need for feeler as well as thinker hymns. Upon examining the book when it came out, I was appalled to discover only token representation of hymns coming from the charismatic renewal, a movement of spiritual vitality. Not only were few renewal hymns added, but several of the older pietist hymns like "What a Friend We Have in Jesus" were removed. As a result, there are relatively few hymns that can be described as feeler hymns. Most hymns are content hymns, not emotive ones. As one disappointed laywoman put it somewhat derisively, "They're comprehensive, all right! The same kind of 'head' hymn as before, only now from fourteen different nationalities."

In one sense the quest for inclusivity was successful. In another sense, the preferred hymn style of a sizable group of people was not honored. Not surprisingly, a substantial number of Episcopal congregations have a second hymnbook in the pews, one of renewal songs.

Bible study to the spiritual thinker is a time to study the doctrinal and ethical truths of the faith. The spiritual thinker wants to know what the truth is, and wants to understand God's plan—for the universe, and for him or herself. Sadly, sometimes this quest is more for the sake of understanding the truth itself than for applying it to the specific situations people are in. Or sometimes the thinker concludes that the only thing that matters is the truth; the way the truth is presented does not matter. "If they don't like it, that's tough," one woman told me. "This is what God says. Period." I agreed with her in that what she was saying was God's truth; but I pointed out that most of the time, at least, it is also possible to give God's truth with God's love.

If the spiritual thinker is also a spiritual sensate, Bible study will likely be led in a straightforward, "What does the text say, and how do we understand what it teaches and do what it demands?" kind of way. With spiritual thinkers who are also spiritual intuitives there may be more speculation, but it is more to expand the mind than the heart.

Spiritual thinkers want the presentation to be logical. God is known, not so much relationally as by His attributes and actions. The teacher must have his or her facts straight and present them in a logical manner, answering questions and carefully refuting false ideas. The thinker function can bring a good balance to those churches that are in danger of rejecting the once-for-all truths of the Gospel because they seem to be exclusionary. The thinker will help remind us that often the truth is tough love, accepted not because it allows us to do what we want, but because it is God's truth, and as such incumbent upon all whom He has created. The image that we may use for the spiritual thinker is that of light illuminating the mind.

Spiritual feelers want to be moved emotionally in a Bible study. They are studying the Bible to learn about their Friend, Jesus. Yes, doctrines and ethics are important, but only because Jesus is their source, not because they are logical or answer fundamental philosophical questions.

When they read in the Bible about how God responds to a hurting person, they tie in more to the hurt of the person and how people similarly hurt today than they do to what this response says about who God is and about the nature of human need. Sometimes a teacher's statement will be accepted more because it feels right than because the teacher was convincing.

If the lesson does not help the spiritual feeler grow in relationship with God or learn how to help others, its relevancy is challenged. The feeler will add to the debate that since God loves even the fallen and rebellious, any presentation of the truth—especially when it is a hard saying—must be loving. Further, the feeler can remind us that we are loved by God even when we fall short of His will.

Sometimes, however, the feeler goes too far with this. Unlike thinkers, many feelers find disharmony difficult to take and will do virtually anything—including compromise the truth—to restore it. I heard one person returning from an annual meeting of her denomination. "We avoided a split," she said. "We had to give in a lot but we kept the family together."

If the giving in was on nonessentials or on areas where biblical Christians may legitimately have significant differences, it was good that the people lovingly humbled themselves for the sake of their brothers and sisters. But if in order to maintain harmony there was compromise on basic truths, this was a sell-out. Jesus never did this. We never read that He came even remotely close to saying, "Pharisees, Sadducees, zealots! Look, why be in disharmony? People are more important than doctrines. Let's forget our differences and live in love." Instead, we find Jesus more than ready to contradict, to oppose and even to divide over basic truths.

Often in adult children of alcoholics (among others), there is a strong tendency to perfectionism. Having grown up in a home where one had to behave exactly in a certain manner—lest it upset the fragile family system—such persons tend to view life and their walk with God as an unrelenting crusade for perfection with nothing but blame for failure. The spiritual feeler can bring the good news that God does not so much want perfection as *He wants us*. By His grace, there is help for us to grow in a way that is graced, not forced, and there is forgiveness for the repentant sinner who does stumble. If the image for the spiritual thinker is light for the mind, that of the spiritual feeler is heat warming the heart. For a Christian to be balanced, of course, there needs to be some of each.

We note this balance in the life and ministry of John Wesley. On May 24, 1738, at a little chapel on Aldersgate Street, London, John Wesley had an experience of God that transformed not only Wesley, but eventually all of England. "I felt my heart strangely warmed," he wrote later. Wesley grabbed in his heart

Free to Be Me!

the truth that Christ had died for his sins and that it was futile to try to earn his salvation through his strivings. *Doctrinally,* Wesley knew that all along, for his mind had been well-illuminated about the Gospel from his parents' teaching and his studies at Oxford. *Emotionally,* Wesley needed his Aldersgate experience to plant that truth in his heart.

The two were vital: Without his education, the Aldersgate experience would have given Wesley a platform of warmth and love that might have made people feel good for a while but would not have changed their lives in a lasting way. Without his Aldersgate experience, Wesley would have continued to teach the doctrines of the faith without power and to embarrass himself and his Lord with his often reckless strivings. Wesley's ministry was so powerful because his ministry was so balanced.

Having said all this, however, seldom is one exactly balanced between spiritual thinking and spiritual feeling. By staying close to other members of the Body of Christ who have the opposite spiritual personality, we can keep ourselves and them from going off into serious imbalance.

Several years ago I witnessed a humorous event involving children and spiritual thinking and feeling. I was taking my elder son, Stephen, then seven, and my daughter Jennifer, then five, on a walking tour of the North End of Boston. We went into St. Leonard's Roman Catholic Church, a very Italian, turn-of-the-century kind of church building. In one corner was a rather gruesome statue, depicting in all its goriness the agony of Christ's crucifixion. Stephen, a feeler, looked at it, turned away, covered his eyes and with great emotion said, "Look at how Jesus suffered when He died for me."

Jennifer, a thinker, pulled herself up to her full height, looked Stephen in the eyes and said, "Stephen, this is where Jesus was paying the penalty price for our sins so that those who put their

190

trust in Him will go to heaven when they die. Stephen, we've had this discussion before!"

Stephen was feeling viscerally the death of his Friend, Jesus, who died for him. Jennifer was giving a learned discourse on substitutionary atonement theology! Both were correct, and both grabbed the truth of what Christ was doing for them, but they grabbed it in different ways. To be sure, as Stephen grew older I explained to him what all of this meant theologically, so that his mind could get on board, too. Nevertheless, Stephen still relates to the atoning death of Christ more from his heart. Jennifer still relates to Jesus' death in a thinker fashion, but I hope she will feel more in her heart the personal agony of Jesus' dying and that this was done, yes, for all sinners, but also *for her personally*.

To have a church that can minister to both the Stephens and the Jennifers of this world, it is necessary to make sure that the prayers, the hymns and the sermons and teachings all take into account the significant differences between spiritual thinkers and spiritual feelers. This—not a misguided attitude of anything goes theologically or morally—is the true meaning of inclusivity.

In evangelism, spiritual thinkers and spiritual feelers conduct themselves differently, thinkers appealing more to the mind and feelers more to the heart. A spiritual thinker is more likely to want to anticipate and answer objections to the faith. He or she is more likely to make use of tracts with the title "Christianity Appeals to the Thinking Man." He or she is more likely to see Christianity as the only philosophy that makes sense of the universe and will try to convince others of this fact.

Spiritual feelers will more likely try to tell people how they can know God personally, how He loves them personally and how this loving, powerful God can take away their hurts and make them feel better inside. Spiritual feelers will often share testimonies of how prayer healed a person or took away the rebellious

Free to Be Me!

attitudes a teenager had raging inside her or saved a marriage, and how these illustrate what God can do for anyone who lets Jesus into his heart.

Obviously we need both kinds of evangelism, since there are both thinkers and feelers to be reached in the world, but again we need to remember to focus on the personality of the one with whom we are sharing the faith. It is no good, for example, for a spiritual thinker to evangelize a hurting housewife with a lofty philosophical discourse when what she wants to know is "Can God take my hurt away?" Nor is it wise for the spiritual feeler to evangelize a spiritually searching graduate student with an invitation to be a sunbeam for Jesus when she has questions about life after death. The point is, as you celebrate the personality God gave you, be appropriately sensitive to the needs *and personalities* of the people to whom you are ministering.

In pastoral care, a spiritual thinker is often likely to provide a truth that the parishioner needs to hear.

Father Charles went to the homes of two widows who were having perpetual money problems. As a spiritual thinker, Charles did not spend much time "holding the hands" of Doris or Ruby, the widows. Instead, he looked around their houses and said, "I think I have an answer to your financial problem. You have no storm windows or doors, and you heat the upstairs even though no one is living there. You have a freezer downstairs that's running but there's little in it. The farmer's market has a sale every Saturday. We can fill your refrigerator—I can loan you the money from my discretionary fund—and you can eat for a whole lot less. I think we've got the problem licked."

I happened to be at Father Charles' church several months later to conduct a three-day healing mission. Both Doris and Ruby were there and eventually they got around to telling me about their priest. Would you believe that, although Doris and Ruby both had the same problem, Doris thought Father Charles was the best clergyman since the apostles while Ruby was in the process of writing to the bishop about that rude, snippy young man.

Doris put it this way: "Father Jonathan, who had been here before, would spend a lot of time feeling sorry for me, but he never helped me. An hour or two of sympathy and he'd be gone and I'd still have my money woes. Oh, he might give me ten dollars to help, but that never solved the problem. This Father Charles is quite the fellow. He solved my poverty problem. I feel I have my dignity back."

That wasn't Ruby's reaction. "Who does he think he is telling me my business? I guess they don't make priests like they used to. Old Father Jonathan, now there was a priest. He'd come out regularly and sit down and have a cup of tea with me and sympathize about my money woes. This new person, I can hardly call him a priest, came out and without so much as a how do you do he's telling me what's wrong with my house. The idea!"

I feel for poor Father Charles. I was once priest of a small church where some in the congregation thanked God that Father So-and-So was no longer there and I was, and a few others wrote to the bishop about me complaining I was not like Father So-and-So. The simple fact is, few people, St. Paul notwithstanding, can be all things to all people, no matter how sensitive we are to their particular needs and personalities.

But then again, we were never meant to be. Ephesians 4:12 describes the job of the pastor/teacher in a congregation as one who equips the saints to do the work of ministry. Rather than one poor overworked individual trying in vain to have all the gifts of the Holy Spirit, carry out all the very different tasks of ministry and match all the personalities of his flock, the pastor/teacher should train and equip his people to minister, deploying them according to their gifts, talents and personalities.

In pastoral counseling, spiritual thinkers often center in on the issue at hand while spiritual feelers often center in on emotions and feelings.

Ruth went through a divorce and went to Pastor Doug for counseling. Pastor Doug had been in the ministry for fifty years and had great wisdom. He sensed that although Ruth had several issues that needed to be discussed—the circumstances of the breakup of her marriage, certain traits she had that likely wounded the marriage and so on—what she needed first was to unload a burden of shame, hurt, rejection and failure. So, although Pastor Doug was more attuned to issues, he was experienced and wise enough to ask Ruth questions oriented around her feelings.

When it comes to the meeting of practical needs, spiritual thinkers attempt to meet the circumstantial need and spiritual feelers attempt to meet the emotional need. Mary and I are learning how to minister pastorally to each other according to the kind of need we have at the moment. I might come home from my work as president of Institute for Christian Renewal and talk about a business problem. Mary might start to suggest practical solutions to the problem, but soon it will be obvious I'm not listening to her suggestions.

Finally, it will dawn on one or both of us that I am not in this instance in need of a practical solution as much as I am in need of some sympathy for the bad day the problem caused me. Sometimes I will even hold up my hand and say, "Thanks for the suggestions, but what I really need is a hug." On other occasions I might be given the hug first and quickly say, "Thanks, that was wonderful, but help me think through the problem."

The same is true for Mary. On one occasion she may need to discuss the problem, on another receive love and sympathy. We are learning how to recognize which need is primary and communicate that to each other. If we forget to do that or can't figure it out, we try to be attuned to each other so we can shift responses as needed.

As most people tend to be better at one than the other, wise is the church that watches for both the circumstantial needs and the emotional needs of its people and engages in ministry to people according to their spiritual gifts and personalities.

In matters of justice, spiritual thinkers see injustice as the violation of standards and rights. God has given certain immutable laws and they have been broken. An injustice has occurred and it must be straightened out. Is it right for black people to be shunted to filthy restrooms while only white people can enter the clean, up-to-date facilities? Is it right for a baby to be killed because a mother wants to claim a selfish right to choose? Spiritual thinkers tend to go from the issue of what is right to the specific instance, from the general law to the individual person.

Spiritual feelers usually work the other way. It is Larry who is denied a job because he is a white male and the local hiring quota demands minorities, no matter how qualified. It is Dorothy who is fired as a flight attendant because she is a few pounds overweight and approaching forty. Spiritual feelers sometimes do not get engaged in matters of justice until someone they know is involved. They will take up the cause because they can feel an individual's pain. Only then will they consider principles of justice. Until they personalize and feel them, concepts like fairness, equality and justice are just abstractions.

Thus, when a church looks at biblical statements of justice, it should look at both the broad principles—What are the issues here?—and the specific instances in the lives of people—Are there people nearby who have been victims of injustice, and can we help them? When getting the church people mobilized to

Free to Be Me!

engage in matters of justice, remember that some will look at issues and some at specific people. Neither one is better or worse than the other. Both are needed.

Judge/Perceiver Spirituality

The difference between the spiritual judge and the spiritual perceiver can best be described as the difference between framework and freedom, or between structure and spontaneity. Spiritual judges profit from spiritual expression that has structure, order, a clearly marked path of steps to be taken, or a specific plan.

At Oxford, John and Charles Wesley and their companions were given the label *Methodist* because of the structured, methodical way they went about their spiritual lives. Spiritual perceivers find all of this confining. They know the Spirit blows where He wills (John 3:8) and one needs to be free to respond accordingly. They also believe that being flexible and spontaneous liberates one to serve God better. St. Francis of Assisi was such a person, and this troubadour for the Lord is held up by spiritual perceivers as one who could freely move from place to place, doing spontaneous acts of kindness, sharing in simple ways the beauty and love of God, and enjoying all of God's creation.

In prayer, a spiritual judge will likely be more structured and organized, especially if also a spiritual sensate. A spiritual perceiver will likely be more spontaneous, especially if also a spiritual intuitive. Spiritual judges will not mind an order of prayer, and will set aside a specific time—often the same time—for prayer. Yes, without some spontaneity the surprises of God can be missed, but spiritual judges point out that the words *disciple* and *discipline* are intimately related.

Spiritual perceivers find structured prayer confining, and, if forced to do it, quickly feel guilty either for not liking it or for failing to carry it through. Better let them wander from one topic to another in prayer. Remind them it is perfectly permissible for them to pray when the thought of prayer pops into their minds. Taking it too far, of course, means the likelihood of an unbalanced spiritual diet, but spiritual perceivers know the freedom found in Jesus' encouragement to take no thought for the morrow (Matthew 6:34).

In worship, spiritual judges like order and spiritual perceivers like flexibility. Spiritual judges remember the Pauline statement that everything be done decently and in order (1 Corinthians 14:40). They know that God is not a God of confusion but of peace (1 Corinthians 14:33). They know that a set liturgical formula can ensure a balanced spiritual diet and that God can direct a worship service months ahead of time just as easily as He can right on the spot.

When I came into the Episcopal Church at age sixteen, I figured out quickly that every Sunday we would have, for certain, prayers about specific things for which the Bible tells us to pray, a confession of sin and assurance of God's forgiveness, Scripture lessons from an assigned lectionary, thereby ensuring that we would hear a large portion of the Word of God over a few years, and so on. In the denomination I had left, the services were generally up to the minister and often some things were overemphasized and others neglected. Like other spiritual judges I preferred to follow a set liturgy every Sunday and take part in a more formal worship service.

Many spiritual perceivers believe that the Holy Spirit can lead in worship in a way far better than human planning can accomplish. They know that a wonderful service, fresh and unique, can occur when God is in charge. They know that in a worship

Free to Be Me!

service God can give prophetic words or can lead someone to start singing a song or share a testimony in response to something that was just taught, prayed, sung or shared. They wonder why some prefer to follow a form when it seems more respectful to God to have a general itinerary and wait upon Him to see what He wants to do. Spiritual perceivers want to be free to respond to the moment, whether by framing a worship service around some momentous event in the country or some specific need in the congregation.

Obviously, there are advantages and disadvantages to both. Structure can give a balanced diet, but it can also stifle. Freedom can allow the Spirit to lead or it can allow poor planning and sloppiness to rule. Dignity can be recognizing the worthiness of God or it can just be a way to keep God from coming too close. Informality can be a celebration of the immanent presence of our God, or it can be a slap-dash, second-best offering.

Many churches are choosing to have several services during the week. A few of these, often midweek and early Sunday morning Communion services, are quite structured. People who like structure find them a blessing, because, as one man told me, "I'm so familiar with what's coming next I can focus on God and not have my attention diverted to what new thing is coming." Other services, such as a weeknight service of prayer and praise, are loosely structured. It takes time to get people to hear the Holy Spirit so that the service is truly led by Him and not just an exercise in winging it, but the results are well worth the effort.

Often the principal Sunday service is a combination, a sort of freedom in a framework. In services like this, there is a specific set order and things are prepared for in advance. But periodically there is space left for a spontaneous response should any be forthcoming. There may, for example, be assigned music at the beginning of the service, but before moving on to what is next in the order of worship, space is left for people to start singing a hymn or chorus spontaneously or request that a certain hymn out of the hymnal be sung. Or, the congregation may pray via a set order of prayer, ensuring the things that should be prayed for are prayed for, but then there is space for people to add their own specific prayers spontaneously as God leads. And at a few times in the liturgy there are appropriate breaks, should there be a prophetic word of the Lord to be shared.

This balance between structure and freedom recognizes that while God does break in, He seldom breaks good order. Seldom is it ever appropriate for a parishioner to stand up in the middle of a sermon and give a prophetic word! On the other hand, it is also unbalanced for a worship service to speak to God without giving Him a chance to speak to His people.

In Bible study, a spiritual judge will more likely prefer a well-prepared, logical presentation of the material, focusing more on content if the judge is also a spiritual thinker, or focusing more on the Person of Jesus if the judge is also a spiritual feeler. In either case—following the Truth or obeying a Friend—the spiritual judge will note the duties and commands that Scripture gives.

The spiritual judge studying alone will often have a plan for study. He or she might, for example, read through the book of Mark in a month, looking up all the names, places and items that are unknowns. While it may be interesting to wander randomly through Scripture to study whatever is interesting at a given moment, that might not give a complete or balanced understanding of the Word of God. In a group, the spiritual judge will get uncomfortable if the discussion strays too far from the topic at hand. He or she usually likes there to be some set goals given and adhered to so that at the end the group can point to what they have accomplished.

Spiritual perceivers, on the other hand, often study more informally. They will sit down one night and open to something that strikes their fancy and read until their fancy shifts. They may read for several hours, and then not read again for days, until something moves them to pick up the Bible again.

Unless what they are reading strikes them, it will not be remembered. Fortunately, such an informal approach allows study to be fun, so there is the likelihood of their fancy being struck often. They know they are more likely to do God's will if it comes from God spontaneously moving them deep within, saying, "Hey, let's do this," than if a formal study concludes, "My bounden duty is. . . ." They don't mind if group study meanders around several topics, as long as it is all interesting.

Wise is the church, therefore, that offers different kinds of Bible studies. For the spiritual judges, the church should have Bible studies with set themes—a systematic study of the book of Romans, for example, or the Scripture passages for the next Sunday service. For the spiritual perceivers, the church should have Bible studies that respond to the needs of the moment.

I know of one church that had a Bible study group with four leaders who alternated every week. Each began with a meditation on a particular Bible passage and related the discussion that followed to some major event in the world that week. Another way to respond to the needs of both groups is to have two Bible studies, one a formal presentation with learning goals and the other an unstructured focus on the text.

In evangelism, the spiritual judges often find carefully structured programs to be helpful. They like for ordered planning of everything that goes into an evangelistic service to which the public is invited. The word *intentional* well describes the evangelistic style of a spiritual judge. It could also be used to describe his or her spirituality in general.

A spiritual perceiver will tend to evangelize on the spur of the moment or as an opportunity presents itself. While this means that those things requiring planning may be left undone, the warm style of a spiritual perceiver is often better received. For those with bad experiences of being grabbed by the lapels and witnessed to by those on a crusade, the informal, relaxed style of a spiritual perceiver is often refreshing.

Pastoral care will also reflect these structured or spontaneous approaches. Spiritual judges will have a formal schedule of visitation and will often have a plan for anticipating various pastoral needs that may occur. In visiting in the home, a spiritual judge is likely to have a specific purpose for the visit and know in advance how long it will be. One pastor, upon arriving at his new church, spent several weeks assessing the needs of his flock using structured interviews and a lengthy questionnaire. From the data, he planned a two-year program of guest speakers, workshops and lay training in those areas where needs were demonstrated.

As with so many other aspects of ministry, some people will respond to this style of pastoral care and others will not. Those responding well to a structured program of pastoral care will compliment the person leading it, because "finally we're looking long-range and anticipating problems before they arise." Those who do not respond well to this style of ministry will lament that "they're putting a program ahead of people."

Spiritual perceivers, true to their informal ways, are always available for the odd five or ten minutes here or there. They will sit down and have a chat. They will visit in the homes in a relaxed, easygoing way. There are advantages and disadvantages to this approach, of course. Some people like the freedom to pick up the telephone and be able to spend five minutes with the pastor virtually at any time. "He's not so busy with planning and committees that he doesn't have time for me," one woman told me about her perceiver pastor. Others lamented that more was not being accomplished.

How do we make use of both styles? By making sure there are both spiritual judges and spiritual perceivers on the pastoral care team. Both have their gifts to offer, their roles to play and their constituencies to reach. Of the two, the judge should be in charge as he or she will most likely have the administrative gifts.

An interesting note from the church growth people: A person with the gift of pastor (probably feeler-perceiver in Myers-Briggs language) will usually have a pastorate of no more than a hundred people or so. If it is larger than that it will likely shrink to that number over the years. The reason is that these warm-hearted leaders are "people-oriented"—they feel it is important to attend personally to needs as they occur—and it is impossible to minister to more than a hundred people in that fashion. Those who respond to this type of ministry will feel well cared for.

Somebody who operates as a visionary and equipper for ministry, however, can preside over a larger congregation. This person will have less contact with the people individually, but will devote his time to long-range planning, finding ways to meet needs, training and deploying people with various gifts, and supervising them in ministry to the people. This will be a growing church.

In the meeting of practical needs, as has been indicated, spiritual judges will plan ahead so needs are anticipated, while spiritual perceivers will respond to needs as they arise.

In matters of justice as well, spiritual judges will ask questions about structures while spiritual perceivers will respond to individual problems as they arise.

Epilogue: How to Make Your Church Personality-Friendly

❖ An awareness of the differences in personality type will enable members of the church to find their niches. As Paul points out in his discussion of the various parts of the Body of Christ in 1 Corinthians 12, no one part can say to another, "We have no need of you." This is true with the gifts of the Holy Spirit. It is also true with the variety of personality types God gives. Within the boundaries of the truth as given in Scripture, there is room for a rich diversity. Members can be encouraged to be themselves, and then grow by God's grace into better versions of that calling. The church leaders can make sure that this rich and biblical diversity is ministered to adequately by providing prayer, worship, study, ministry instruction, training and other expressions that take into account the different preferences, styles and orientations the members have.

Our churches can be personality-friendly. If they are, they will help heal some of the personality wounds the members have, and enhance spiritual growth. They will say to the world that one does not have to forsake one's personality to become a Christian,

Free to Be Me!

just one's sin. And they will train their members to go to the different kinds of people in this broken and hurting world and meet them with the redemption that is offered in Christ.

What can we do to have a personality-friendly church? That is to say, if we recognize that within the boundaries of the Gospel there is room for a rich diversity, how do we make our local congregations expressive of that balance? I believe there are a number of things we can do. What follows are general suggestions. You will need God's guidance in making specific applications to your unique situation.

First, we can pray, asking that God both move hearts and informs minds. Only God can get us fallen creatures to live in balance. Only He can give us the wisdom of how to proceed.

Second, we can instruct the congregation in the principle of the freedom of expression within the framework of orthodoxy. For many, this will be a new concept.

Third, we can inform the people as to the variety of personality types and how each of these brings a specific gift and a specific problem to the matter of spiritual expression. Have a personality type and personal growth weekend at your church. Hold up before the congregation examples, from Scripture and Church history, of people with different spiritual types.

Fourth, we can encourage the church members by word and example to make their congregation a truth-in-love place where people may grow in Christ. We can strive for the goal of making our fellowships places where sins will be lovingly corrected and where people can try out different forms of spiritual expression, being free to make mistakes as they do. We must work intentionally toward reaching that goal.

Fifth, we can make available a number of Bible studies, prayer groups, worship services and ministry projects that reflect the variety of spiritual personality types we looked at in the final chapter. In other words, it is not good enough to inform people that there are a number of ways to study, pray, worship and serve; we must make these accessible.

Sixth, we can ask people who are familiar with these various offerings to help coach those for whom they are new. When people try out a new style of Bible study, for example, they may need help in making it their own. Someone who can show them how it might meet their needs is an asset.

Seventh, we can train workers in the ministry of inner healing. As people start to realize they can truly be themselves in our churches, many of them will also become more aware of the pain within themselves. This seems ironic at first—the more friendly the church becomes the more some members feel they are in pain—until we realize that for many years people have been either emotionally numb or emotionally calloused. Now with the hope that they can be themselves, they may need first to confront their woundedness and get that healed before they can enjoy a new, more authentic way of living.

Appendix 1: Releasing Anger, Pain and Judgment: Healing Relationships for Christians

J. Douglas Sholl, D.Min.*

❖ God wants to free us from emotional reactions and judgments by working through our prayers and friends in the following ways:

1. Let the Spirit of truth help reveal and identify our hurts, angers and judgments. Come out of denial into God's light (1 John 1:5-10).

2. Get in touch with our feelings and judgments. Experience them. Own them. Admit that they are still a part of our lives. We are no longer split off from them.

3. Find a trusted brother(s) and/or sister(s) to share these with. Express and confess what was hidden. Rather than giving

---

* This section is copyright © 1988 by J. Douglas Sholl, D.Min., and used with permission.

Appendix 1: Releasing Anger, Pain and Judgment

these feelings power, this will help us master/control/release them (James 5:16).

4. Allow feelings and judgments to be accepted/affirmed/validated by Christian friends. Remember that the original emotional reaction was not unusual.

5. Also remember that we are accountable for how we deal with these judgments and feelings. Take an inventory of any damage that they have promoted in our lives or in the lives of others. Confess (Matthew 7:1ff; Galatians 6:7-10; Hebrews 12:15).

6. Let the Spirit of grace and supplication bring godly sorrow and repentance for damaged relationships with self, others and God.

7. Let the Holy Spirit show us Jesus. Release the feelings and judgments to Jesus. Give Him everything that has caused damage so He can place it all on the cross where it belongs.

8. Receive God's forgiveness and cleansing. Ask the Holy Spirit to fill the empty places with spiritual fruit.

9. Forgive the one(s) who hurt us, as Christ has forgiven us and set us free (Ephesians 4:32).

10. Exonerate the one(s) who hurt us. Acknowledge their weaknesses and limitations. Jesus has paid the full price for their sins, including the ones directed toward us. He has canceled their debts. We are free from entitlements and grudges. We are free to be pleasing to God and to ourselves.

Appendix 2: Objections to Personality Type Theory

❖ Should a Christian engage in the study of personality types? Recently there have been a number of books and articles by Christian authors critical of the subject. While I do not share their total rejection of the subject of personality type, they do raise issues that we need to look at briefly.

One objection raised by opponents of personality type theory is that its origins are occultic. They point out that the four-temperament theory of personality (sanguine, choleric, melancholic and phlegmatic), later explored by Tim LaHaye, derives from ancient Greek astrology. They note that the personality type theory popularized as the Myers-Briggs Type Indicator comes from Carl Jung, who admitted that some of his insights came to him while he was engaged in occult practices. Therefore, say the objectors, we must reject the whole theory as occultic.

My response is that both medicine and baklava also came from ancient Greece; but we don't reject them because of their origins! Put more delicately, we need accept neither the origins of personality type theory nor any unbiblical aspects of the theory in

Appendix 2: Objections to Personality Type Theory

order to accept those aspects that *do* square with the truth. We gladly receive the benefits of modern medicine, even though aspects of it have, at times, been intertwined with the occult and though many of its discoveries were made by nonbelievers. The tunes of some of the hymns we sing—"A Mighty Fortress is Our God," for example—were used originally for profane tavern ditties. Do we stop singing them because their origins are tainted? The apostle Paul quoted pagan poets and made use of pagan philosophical arguments to explain Christian truths without adopting pagan belief systems.

As with any idea or system of thought, we should run the various personality type theories through the filter of Scripture, straining out what is incompatible and accepting the rest. I have found that while I, as a biblical Christian, would take issue with a few things these temperament or personality type theories have to say, most of their assertions are true to Scripture and therefore true to life.

A second objection is that in some churches the study of personality type has become a substitute Gospel. I agree! There are many churches that have long ago given up on historic, biblical Christianity for religious modernism. This is not a judgment on my part. These churches readily and proudly admit this. The trouble is, without the Gospel there has to be something in its place. What usually happens is a steady parade of the latest theological, political or psychological fads. I have seen churches go through phases of whatever is the next Gospel substitute.

But we need not do this in order to receive the benefits that a study of personality type has to offer. We can be centered in the historic, changeless truths of the Gospel, and thank God that, as with the study of modern medicine, electricity, the automobile and the like, there are new insights into human personality from which we can profit.

Appendix 2: Objections to Personality Type Theory

One of the many problems in making personality type theory a substitute Gospel is that by not relying on the empowerment of the Holy Spirit, we can miss His creative surprises: Sometimes He works through us in ways *opposite* to our personalities. Many have shared with me something I found out years ago. When we minister under the anointing of the Holy Spirit, we often do things far beyond our own abilities and different from our normal way of being.

In my book *Christian Healing*, I mentioned a woman named Bertha (pages 188-189 and 197). In day-to-day life Bertha seems to lack even basic common sense, but when she ministers under the power of the Holy Spirit, God gives her the gift called the word of wisdom and Bertha comes out with the most incredibly wise statements!

So while personality type theory may sometimes predict the kinds of ministry in which we will engage, or describe the way in which we will go about those ministries (an introvert will probably evangelize more quietly than an extravert), we have to be careful not to place ourselves—or God!—in a box here. An introvert deacon from Florida, who finds her ministry bearing the most fruit when the Holy Spirit enables her to minister in an extraverted way, wrote me recently: "One of the sure signs to me that I am not flowing with the energizing of the Spirit is the tendency to withdraw into myself and avoid people interaction."

Third, personality types have become the new astrology, placing people in bondage to yet another deterministic system. That is, they say, *everything* that can be said about a person is done by describing his or her personality type, about which nothing can be changed. Everyone is helpless, therefore, before an impersonal, intractable fate.

There is truth to this objection also. I have seen people make excuses for their bad behavior because of their personality type.

211

Appendix 2: Objections to Personality Type Theory

("I can't help it. You know how we extraverts are.") I have seen people make horrible generalizations, lumping everyone together irrespective of their own unique differences. ("Let's get Larry to do this job. He's a sanguine and all sanguines are good at this sort of thing.") I have seen people counseled not to get married because "we all know ENFPs and ISTJs just can't make it as a couple."

But once again, just because there are simplistic understandings and inappropriate applications of the theory does not mean there is no truth to it. You know what I mean: Just because the occasional physician is convicted of malpractice does not mean we give up on scientific medicine. As a Christian, I would say that while our personality type may nudge us toward *expressing* sinful attitudes or orientations in a particular way, it does not make us sin or excuse us for sinning.

Regarding the marriage question, there is a big difference between diverse personality types and diverse character. While the couple's personality types may indicate—as they did for Mary and me—some of the likely areas of conflict, that does not mean that certain personality types should not marry people of certain other personality types. Although the areas of likely harmony and disharmony will differ, *any* combination of personality types, including two people of the same personality type, will have bane and blessing.

As an aside, let me stress that this is why we should make sure that anyone who is going to use these temperament or personality type assessment tools is professionally trained and qualified. An important part of the training in psychological instruments is to know their limitations and their potential misuses. Armchair or pop psychologists usually lack both the training and the intellectual depth to appreciate the difference between appropriate and inappropriate uses of psychological tools.

Similar to this is the fourth objection, that to talk about personality type is to stereotype and prejudge people. There is truth to this objection. It is axiomatic in Myers-Briggs circles that "all ENFJs are similar in many ways and each ENFJ is unique in his or her own way." John Ackerman puts it like this: The Myers-Briggs Type Indicator is like a zip code, not giving the exact address but helping people find the right state, city and neighborhood (*Cherishing Our Differences*). In other words, it gives helpful information but it does not label every individual.

In addition, while personality type helps us understand something about a person, we also learn much from spiritual gifts, birth order, the number of siblings, a childhood of poverty or wealth, one's ethnic background, whether one is male or female and the role expectations this brings, the presence or absence of serious childhood illness and frequent family moves. There is much we can gain from a study of personality type as long as we remember it is but one way of understanding a person.

A fifth objection is that many in ministry are using personality type theory as a self-help program when true personal growth and success in ministry must come by the grace of God. Once again, I have seen this happen. But that is the fault of those who, whatever the insight or program, insist on human self-improvement or human effort and wisdom to grow in ministry rather than a humble waiting on the Lord for empowerment. It is not the fault of personality type theory.

While noting that personal growth and success in ministry do not depend solely on us, however, we should not run to the opposite pole. Scripture describes personal growth as a cooperative venture between God and man. When Scripture tells us, "Work out [the implications of] your salvation with fear and trembling, for it is God who works in you" (Philippians 2:12-13), we are instructed both to do our part and to let God do His.

Appendix 2: Objections to Personality Type Theory

We find something similar in terms of ministry. Paul reminded his disciple Timothy of two important truths to be grasped if Timothy was ever to exercise good leadership. One was that Timothy needed to stir up the gift within him that he received when Paul laid hands on him (2 Timothy 1:6). The other was that Timothy had to work diligently to be able to handle in a right way the word of truth (2 Timothy 2:15). Once again, a cooperative effort between God and man: Timothy needed both to rely on divine empowerment and to do his homework. God's part, our part. I believe that the insights of personality type theory can be one aspect—please note, *one* aspect—of informing us as to what our part is.

The fruit of the Holy Spirit—love, joy, peace, patience, kindness, goodness, faithfulness, gentleness, self-control (Galatians 5:22-23)—is the same for everyone, *but it can be manifested in different ways* according to personality.

Lastly, it is said that we do not find temperament or personality type teaching in Scripture. We might ask the question, "Do we have to in order for it to be valid?" To be a Scripture-based Christian does not mean that everything has to be in the Bible in order for us to accept it as true. Rather, it means that whatever is proposed as truth cannot be accepted if Scripture contradicts it. In other words, we do not have to see personality type theory in the Bible in order for it to be received as true; we just have to make sure that the Bible doesn't rule it out. Otherwise, won't we be like the Amish, freezing ourselves in time and never admitting *anything* new? Christians accept medicines, not because the chemical formulae are found in Scripture, but because these medicines are efficacious and are not forbidden in the Bible. Why not personality type theories? If they are not ruled out in Scripture, and to the degree they are true, let us gratefully accept their insights.

Appendix 2: Objections to Personality Type Theory

There *is* some scriptural warrant for studying personality type, even though it is subtle. I believe a careful reading of Scripture will demonstrate that God not only gives different personality types, but that the *style* of a person's ministry will differ accordingly.

We see in the major figures of the New Testament how God chose people of different personalities to carry out His work. There's the down-to-earth, no-nonsense Peter; there's the intellectual yet emotional Paul; there's the mystical John; there's the cautious Timothy; there's the skeptical Thomas. Each had a role to play, and each had his own unique style. While the content of their messages was the same, the way in which each carried out his ministry was shaped by his individual personality.

We see this reflected further in various New Testament writings. The Gospel of Matthew presents Jesus as the new Moses, giving the laws of God. Matthew also shows how Jesus was both the continuation and fulfillment of Old Testament teaching and practice. This is not surprising, for the author of this Gospel was both a Jew and a (presumably) logical, detail-oriented tax collector. The Gospel of Mark is a simple, straightforward presentation of the events of Jesus' adult life. This is not surprising when we realize Mark was scribe to Peter (whose Gospel the Gospel of Mark really is), and the New Testament description of Peter is that of a straightforward man of action. The Gospel of Luke reflects detailed observations; again, not surprising, for Luke was the beloved physician and we would expect physicians to notice details. John's Gospel is that of a serene mystic, with meditations on theological concepts (see the first fourteen verses, for example).

Some people have even suggested that the four Gospels each represent a different personality type. I wonder if one of the reasons God gave us four Gospels is because they present the

Appendix 2: Objections to Personality Type Theory

same truth but in different ways. No matter what our personality type, there is a Gospel that is similar to the way we express ourselves and relate to the world.

When God goes to work making us holier people, He does not destroy the personality we have, He transforms it. Look at Simon Peter. In the Gospels we see that his outgoing, just-the-facts-ma'am personality got him into trouble. He often opened his mouth just to put his foot in it. He could not grasp the complex idea of Jesus having to go to the cross for our sins, so he tried to talk Jesus out of it. The Peter of the Gospels is spiritually immature. But in the Acts of the Apostles, by which time the Holy Spirit has accomplished some spiritual growth in Peter, we don't suddenly find an introvert mystic. We find the same extravert, plain-spoken man, *but with maturity*. God didn't give Peter a different personality. God *improved* the personality He had already given him.*

It is important to recognize this because most of us don't like our personalities. We see how we make fools of ourselves as well as hurt others. We wonder wrongly if the reason we have been wounded is that we somehow deserved it, given who we are. We wonder if our problems are so much a part of us that we will never be different or act differently.

The response God gives to this way of thinking is this: "My child, I gave you this personality as My special gift. I knew you before I formed you in your mother's womb [Jeremiah 1:5; Psalm 139:13]. Just as your eye color and the shape of your ears are a

---

* For an in-depth study in how God transforms rather than destroys the temperament or personality He gave you, see Tim LaHaye's book *Transformed Temperaments*. Along with other books on the same general subject by LaHaye, this book will help you realize that God wants to attend to your wounded personality, not take it away and give you another one, but heal it and make it mature.

part of how I made you, so is your personality. It is something I gave you; thus, there is no personality type that is better or worse than another. Any personality type can be used for My glory or can be an expression of rebellion to Me. Yes, you have misused it. You need to come to Me for forgiveness and you need to let the Holy Spirit mature you. Yes, it has been wounded because of the sin of others. I don't want to give you a different personality. If you were supposed to have a different personality, I would have given you that one in the first place. What I want to do is make you a better version of who you already are. I want to love you, forgive you, heal you and mature you—for your enjoyment, My glory and the sake of the world My Son came to redeem."

And God will do those very things for you, as you let the Holy Spirit work healing and maturation in you.

Bibliography

Personality Type and Temperament

Please Understand Me: Character & Temperament Types by Drs. David Keirsey and Marilyn Bates. A comprehensive overview of personality type theory with applications to marriage, raising children, leadership and teaching. Contains detailed descriptions of each of the sixteen personality types identified in the Myers-Briggs theory, plus the Keirsey Temperament Sorter, a self-scoring personality inventory similar to the Myers-Briggs Type Indicator. Prometheus Nemesis Book Company.

God's Gifted People: Discovering and Using Your Spiritual and Personal Gifts by the Rev. Dr. Gary L. Harbaugh. A basic introduction to the Myers-Briggs Type Indicator with applications to friendship, marriage, families, work, church life and life in general. Augsburg Publishing House.

Prayer and Temperament: Different Prayer Forms for Dif-

ferent Personality Types by Msgr. Chester P. Michael and Marie C. Norrisey. Recommendations of different forms of prayer appropriate for the different temperaments and personality types. A variety of prayer projects are given. The Open Door, Inc.

Personality and Spiritual Freedom: Growing in the Christian Life through Understanding Personality Type and the Myers-Briggs Type Indicator by Robert and Carol Ann Faucett. A basic introduction to typology and its relationship to spiritual development. An Image Book (Doubleday).

Who We Are Is How We Pray: Matching Personality and Spirituality by Dr. Charles J. Keating. Suggests a variety of spiritualities that may be more conducive to spiritual growth given one's personality type. Twenty-Third Publications.

Prayer and Different Types of People by the Rev. Christopher Bryant. Gives a variety of prayer styles for people of different personality types. Center for Applications of Psychological Type.

People Types and Tiger Stripes: A Practical Guide to Learning Styles by Dr. Gordon Lawrence. Application of personality type theory to education. Center for Applications of Psychological Type.

Transformed Temperaments by Dr. Tim LaHaye. Using the ancient Greek four-temperament theory, the author argues that God does not favor one temperament over another, and wishes to transform, not change, a person's temperament. Tyndale House Publishers.

Bibliography

I Love You, But Why Are We So Different? by Dr. Tim LaHaye. Since so many people marry persons of opposite temperament, how can an understanding of temperament enhance marital happiness and resolve marital conflicts? Harvest House Publishers.

Inner Healing

Five Loaves and Two Fishes by Phoebe Cranor. Practical assistance for those seeking inner healing to locate the painful areas of their pasts, offer them to Jesus and experience transformation. Paulist Press.

Healing for Damaged Emotions by the Rev. Dr. David A. Seamands. A veteran United Methodist missionary, pastor and seminary professor shares his insights on the healings of a variety of emotional difficulties. Scripture Press Publishers, Inc.

Putting Away Childish Things by the Rev. Dr. David A. Seamands. How God can change childish behavior patterns that hinder us from growing up in Christ. Victor Books.

Christian Healing: A Practical, Comprehensive Guide by the Rev. Canon Mark A. Pearson. An introductory, overview book on the theory and practice of Christian healing. Chapter 6 deals with the healing of memories. Chosen Books.

My Father's Child—Help and Healing for the Victims of Emotional, Sexual, and Physical Abuse by Lynda D. Elliott and Dr. Vicki L. Tanner. The authors are Christian counselors. Wolgemuth & Hyatt, Publishers, Inc.

Biblical Inner Healing by the Rev. Dr. F. Earle Fox. An explanation of the biblical roots of the healing of memories, a biblical understanding of the unconscious and other foundation stones for a biblically based psychology. Emmaus Ministries.

Healing the Hidden Self by Barbara Shlemon, R.N. Six major stages of development—conception and life in the womb, birth, infancy, childhood, adolescence, young adulthood and adulthood—are discussed, showing how emotional hurt and damage to the inner self is possible, damage that may not manifest until much later. Practical, useful help toward setting people free. Ave Maria Press.

The Transformation of the Inner Man by John Loren and Paula Sandford. The most comprehensive book on inner healing in print. Victory House.

Healing the Wounded Spirit by John Loren and Paula Sandford. Chapters on a whole variety of things that cause or express emotional hurts, such as anorexia, rejection, depression, frustration. Chapters on problems in the womb and intergenerational problems. Victory House.

Healing Victims of Sexual Abuse by Paula Sandford. Love, acceptance and healing to all the victims—the abused, the abuser and their families. A valuable tool for those who minister. Victory House.

Making Peace with Your Inner Child by Rita Bennett. Dealing with the conscious and subconscious record of the emotions, hurts and bad experiences of the childhood years. Fleming H. Revell Company.

Bibliography

Alcoholism and Co-Dependency by Alexander de John. Subjects covered: The Church's response to the alcoholic and his/her family; the needs of adult children of alcoholics; abstinence vs. moderation; intervention; adolescent alcohol abuse; treatment programs. Tyndale House.

Broken Things—Why We Suffer by M. R. de Haan. Applies biblical principles to the issues of tragedy and illness. Can be a source of comfort to those who seek reasons for their suffering. Author explains how brokenness can prepare a person for maturity in his/her walk with Christ, and why being broken is a sign of God's working to refine the potential He sees in His children. Discovery House.

Jesus the Healer by Lloyd John Ogilvie. Exposition of Scripture passages that focus on the nature of healing, wholeness and healthy life experience, with instructions as to how to request and receive God's healing grace. Includes encouragement to become a part of a Christian community that facilitates the healing experience. Fleming H. Revell Company.

A Hunger for Healing by J. Keith Miller. The author shows that the Twelve Steps offer a model for Christian discipleship and spiritual maturity from which all Christians, even those free of evident addiction, can benefit. He suggests that the presence of spiritual and emotional pain, anxiety and confusion in one's life may be indicative of the same spiritual problem found at the heart of alcoholism and other addictions. Each of the Twelve Steps is related to appropriate biblical passages. HarperCollins Publishers.

Serenity—A Companion for 12-Step Recovery. Contains entire New Testament, Psalms and Proverbs. Additionally, there are 84 meditations, seven for each of the Twelve Steps. Each step is explained in the context of scriptural principles.

For Further Information

The *Institute for Christian Renewal,* led by the Rev. Canon Mark A. Pearson, exists to assist individuals and local churches in experiencing the riches Christ offers and in serving effectively in His name. The Institute has a variety of resources for training and equipping people in the ministry of Christian healing, and sponsors Canon Pearson as he travels to churches around the world to conduct teaching workshops, healing missions, training programs and Myers-Briggs retreats.

You can contact the Institute at: ~~148 Plaistow Rd., Plaistow, NH 03865, (603) 382-0273~~. *see front inside cover*

Information and materials about the *Myers-Briggs Type Indicator* are available from the Center for Applications of Psychological Type (CAPT), 2720 N.W. 6th Street, Gainesville, FL 32609, (800) 777-2278.

Information about training workshops is available through Association for Psychological Type (APT), 9140 Ward Parkway, Kansas City, MO 64114, (816) 444-3500. They also offer two publications. One is *Bulletin of Psychological Type* (abbreviated BPT), which is the newsletter of the APT. The second is *Journal of Psychological Type* (JPT), the official research journal of the APT. Those wishing to communicate directly with the editor of JPT may write or telephone: *Journal of Psychological Type,* Department of Psychology, Box 6161, Mississippi State University, Mississippi State, MS 39762, (601) 325-7655.

Bibliography

A variety of Myers-Briggs publications and books are available through APT and also through Consulting Psychologists Press, Inc., 3803 E. Bayshore Road (P.O. Box 10096), Palo Alto, CA 94303-0979, (800) 624-1765. An abbreviated personality assessment instrument similar to the MBTI is the Keirsey Temperament Sorter and is found in the book *Please Understand Me: Character and Temperament Types* by David Keirsey and Marilyn Bates.